East and South East Asian History

Fr. Peter Samuel Kucer, MSA

En Route Books & Media, LLC
St. Louis, MO, USA

En Route Books and Media, LLC
5705 Rhodes Avenue
St. Louis, MO 63109

Cover credit: TJ Burdick

Library of Congress Control Number: 2017956387

Copyright © 2019 Peter Samuel Kucer

ISBN-10: 0-9994704-2-6
ISBN-13: 978-0-9994704-2-8

No part of this booklet may be reproduced, stored in a retrieval system, or transmitted in any form, or by any means, electronic, mechanical, photocopying, or otherwise, without the prior written permission of the author.

DEDICATION

In memory of my mother, Roberta Kucer, who instilled in me a love of study and a love of her people, the chosen people.

In addition, I dedicate this book to the members of my community, the Missionaries of the Holy Apostles.

ACKNOWLEDGMENTS

I would particularly like to acknowledge Fr. Isaac Martinez, MSA, former General of the Missionaries of the Holy Apostles, who gave me permission to publish, and Bishop Christian Rodembourg, MSA, who as the first MSA to be ordained a bishop brought our MSA charism into a deeper ecclesial dimension by assuming the office of bishop the year this book was published. Special thanks to Dr. Sebastian Mahfood, OP, president of En Route Books and Media, for publishing this work.

CONTENTS

Chapter 1: Asian Prehistory 6
Ancient Asian Cultures 6
Quiz 1 11

Chapter 2: East Asian Bronze Age 13
Xia Dynasty 14
Shang Dynasty 17
South East Asian Bronze Age 20
Quiz 2 21

Chapter 3: East Asian Iron Age 23
Zhou Dynasty 23
Mandate from Heaven 25
Xunzi and Mencius 29
Legalism 31
Legalism and Warfare 31
A Catholic Response to Legalism 35
Quiz 3 36

Chapter 4: Early Diversification of East Asian Civilization . 39
Han Dynasty 40
Emperor Wu of the Western Han Dynasty 40
Wang Mang of the Xin Dynasty 41
Ban Zhao of the Eastern Han Dynasty 42
Diversification of East Asian Cultures 48

Funan 49
Champa 51
Chenla 53
Khmer Kingdom 53
Vietnam 54
Quiz 4 56

Chapter 5: East Asia: Foreign Conquest and Influence 59
Mongol Rule in China and Korea 59
Mongol Invasions into South East Asia 61
Islam in the Malay World 63
Western Trade, Christianity and East Asia 67
Quiz 5 76

Chapter 6: Trade and Evangelization (1400s-1700s) 77
European Explorers in Search for the Orient 79
Trade and Colonization 84
Catholic Missionaries 86
Quiz 6 95

Chapter 7: Western Imperialism (1800s-1900s) 97
The British in Asia 98
The French in Asia 102
The U.S. in Asia 105
The Russians in Asia 112
Quiz 7 113

Chapter 8: East Asian Nationalism 115
China and the Boxer Rebellion 116
Japan and the Fall of the Shogunate 120
Korea and Isolationism 123
South East Asian Colonies and Nationalism 125
Quiz 8 126

Chapter 9: East Asia and the West – Rejection, Assimilation, Transformation 129
Korea's Response to Western Culture 129
China's Response to Western Culture 135
Japan's Response to Western Culture 138
South East Asia's Diverse Response to Western Culture 141
Quiz 9 145

Chapter 10: Modern East Asian Imperialism 147
Japan's Imperial Rule 148
The Japanese Empire During World War II 152
The Japanese Empire Ends 154
Quiz 10 158

Chapter 11: East Asia Post World War II 159
Post World War II Japan 160
The Korean War 169
The Vietnam War and Cambodia 172
Quiz 11 178

Chapter 12: Modern East Asia 181
Asian Tigers 181
China: Mao Ze Dong and Deng Xiaoping 184
North Korea and Vietnam 190
Quiz 12 193

Fr. Peter Samuel Kucer, MSA

¹ Statue of Our Lady of La Vang in Ao dai at Phát Diệm Cathedral in La Vang, Vietnam, purported Marian apparition 1798, not recognized by the Holy See. Image courtesy of Wikipedia, https://commons.wikimedia.org/wiki/File:VN_Phat_Diem_tango7174.jpg

Chapter 1: Asian Prehistory

Introduction

Throughout this book, we will study Asian history. The geographic land mass called Asia was originally identified by Europeans in their attempt to understand the world by defining boundaries. From ancient Greek times that pre-dated the birth of Christ, Europeans divided the world into at least two parts: Asia and Europe.[2] Sometimes, Africa was also identified as a separate region. These two parts were named the occident and the orient.[3] The term occident comes from the Latin word *occidentem*, from the verb *occidere* meaning to go down. The noun *occidentem* refers to the western sky "in which the sun sets."[4] Similarly, the term orient originates from Latin. It comes from the Latin word *orientem* which is based on *orire* meaning to rise. The noun

---

[2] Europe is named after a princess in Greek mythology named Europa who Zeus took after he appeared to her as a white bull. Similarly, the name Asia is also found in Greek mythology. Asia is the name of a Titan Goddess.

[3] Barbara A. Weightman, *Dragons and Tigers: A Geography of South, East, and Southeast Asia*, 3rd Edition (Hoboken: John Wiley & Sons, Inc., 2011), 4.

[4] "Occident," Online Etymology Dictionary, http://www.etymonline.com/index.php?allowed_in_frame=0&search=occident&searchmode=none, (accessed November 1, 2015).

orientem refers to that eastern sky "where the sun rises."[5] Below is a map of Asia and all its sub regions.

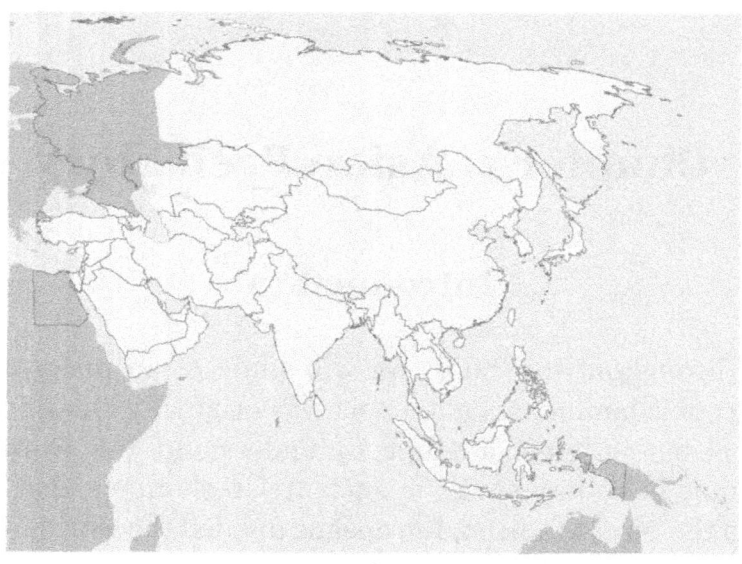

In this book, we will limit our study of Asia to East Asia and South East Asia. Due to the limited nature of our book, we will not study, except in passing, countries of Western Asia, Central Asia, and South Asia. The countries that make up East Asia are China, Taiwan, Japan, Mongolia, North Korea, and South Korea. The countries that comprise South

---

[5] "Orient," Online Etymology Dictionary, http://www.etymonline.com/index.php?allowed_in_frame=0&search=orient&searchmode=none, (accessed November 1, 2015).

[6] historicair 20:13, 20 November 2006 (UTC), "Asia Blank map. The continental boundary to Europe follows the mainstream convention along the Urals, the Ural River, and the crest of the Greater Caucasus (note that the northernmost tip of Azerbaijan is actually north of the Caucasus watershed, but is indicated as part of Asia in this map)," map, https://www.commons.wikimedia.org/wiki/File:Asie.svg, (accessed November 1, 2015).

East Asia are Vietnam, Cambodia, Brunei, Indonesia, Laos, Malaysia, Myanmar (also known as Burma), Philippines, Singapore, Thailand, and East Timor.

In the midst of a vast variety of differences, each of these East Asian regions can be considered as sharing common philosophies, customs, and practices that give each region a specific character. The two regions also share much in common. For this reason, we will study them together while respecting their uniqueness. One of the most obvious differences between the two East Asian regions, as is immediately evident in the maps below, is their geographic location. Unlike East Asia, South East Asia is practically surrounded and divided by water. A common South East Asian phrase that summarizes how the sea unites South East Asians is, "The sea unites and the land divides." The tropical climate with its lengthy periods of rain in South East Asia is also a factor that has shaped South East Asia into a distinct world region. These two geographic aspects have had a profound influence on the South East cultures and have greatly helped to distinguish them from their northern neighbors.[7]

East Asia	South East Asia

8	9

---

[7] Craig Lockard, *Societies, Networks, and Transitions: A Global History* (Boston: Houghton Mifflin Company, 2008), 91.

[8] "East Asia," map, https://commons.wikimedia.org/wiki/

We will begin our study of these Asian regions with a brief overview of their pre-history. One way of delineating the time frame of pre-history is by the absence and then presence of recorded history. History began to be recorded after forms of writing were invented. Since some civilizations began recording their history earlier than others, the time frame of the pre-historical age differs from region to region. It was during the Bronze age that pre-history ended in a few civilizations. After inventing ways to write, these civilizations then used their writing ability to record history.

In Mesopotamia, which is formed out of two Greek words meaning "between two rivers" (the Tigris and the Euphrates), cuneiform was used, and in Egypt hieroglyphs were invented.[10] The word cuneiform comes from the Latin *cuneus* means "a wedge, wedge shaped thing."[11] The word was used in reference to early Mesopotamian writing since it was written with wedge-shaped instruments.

The English word hieroglyphs is also formed out of two Greek words, *hieros* meaning sacred and *glyphein* meaning

---

File%3AEast_Asia_(orthographic_projection).svg (accessed October 28, 2015).

[9] Keepscases, "South East Asia," map, https://www.commons.wikimedia.org/wiki/File%3ASoutheast_Asia_(orthographic_projection).svg, (accessed October 28, 2015).

[10] Gretchen Wildwood, and Rupert Matthews, *Ancient Mesopotamian Civilization* (New York: The Rosen Publishing Group, 2010), 40-41; James P. Allen, *Middle Egyptian: An Introduction to the Language and Culture of Hieroglyphs* (Cambridge: Cambridge University Press, 2014), 1.

[11] "Cuneiform," Online Etymology Dictionary, http://www.etymonline.com/index.php?allowed_in_frame=0&search=cuneiform&searchmode=none, (accessed November 2, 2015).

to carve.¹² Egyptian hieroglyphs appeared about 3250 years ago.¹³ Sometime afterwards, history began to be recorded during the Bronze age, which we will study in the following chapter. In this chapter, we will focus our attention on the early human presence in Eastern Asia. Written history, and other types of documentary evidence, is not the only data that historians use when studying a particular historical era. Material objects that people left behind known as artifacts also are collected and studied. You will be introduced to some of these findings in the next section. Archaeologists often rely on radiocarbon dating in order to determine the age of a particular find.

Sumerian Cuneiform c. 2500s BC

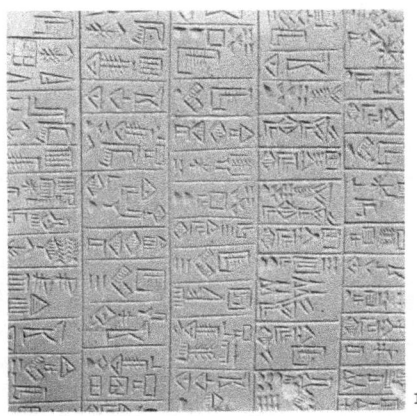
14

---

¹² "Hieroglyphic," Online Etymology Dictionary, http://www.etymonline.com/index.php?term=hieroglyphic&allowed_in_frame=0, (accessed October 19, 2015).

¹³ James P. Allen, *Middle Egyptian: An Introduction to the Language and Culture of Hieroglyphs* (Cambridge: Cambridge University Press, 2014), 2.

¹⁴ Unknown author, "Schøyen Collection MS 3029. Sumerian inscription on a creamy stone plaque, 9,2x9,2x1,2 cm, 6+6 columns, 120 compartments of archaic monumental cuneiform

Fr. Peter Samuel Kucer, MSA

Hieroglyphs - Papyrus of Ani c. 1250 BC

Ancient Asian Cultures

In the Zhiren cave located in southern China, part of a jaw and two molars of early humans (*Homo sapiens*) were discovered. Paleoanthropologists dated these findings to around 100,000 years from the present. A similar finding was discovered in a cave of central China called the Huanglong Cave. Here, teeth that seem likely to have belonged to early human beings were found. The oldest was

---

script by an expert scribe... The text is a list of "gifts from the High and Mighty of Adab to the High Priestess, on the occasion of her election to the temple," Image, https://commons.wikimedia.org/wiki/File%3ASumerian_26th_c_Adab.jpg (accessed October 21, 2015).

[15] En:user:Flembles, Bridgeman Art Library v. Corel Corp. "Cursive hieroglyphs from the Papyrus of Ani, an example of the Egyptian Book of the Dead," photograph, https://www.commons.wikimedia.org/wiki/File%3APapyrus_Ani_curs_hiero.jpg (accessed October 21, 2015).

also dated to 100,000 years from the present.¹⁶

Once these remains belonged to a people of a very early Neolithic Chinese culture. One particularly well-known Neolithic culture is the Yangshao culture (5000 to 3000 BC). The people of this ancient culture settled down in the Yellow River valley. The Yellow River is the second longest river in China. The longest river is the Yangtze River, also known as the Chang Jiang River. The Yellow River obtained its name after the huge amount of silt that is suspended in the river, giving it a yellow glimmer. Not surprisingly, the earliest Chinese communities settled around China's largest rivers both originating from Northern China's Tibetan Plateau.¹⁷ According to some Chinese historians, Chinese culture originated in the valley of the Yellow River out of the Yangshao culture. Other historians argue that while the Yangshao culture certainly contributed to the formation of a distinctly Chinese civilization it was not the sole source.¹⁸

When settled, the Yangshao people learned to grow millet and to raise livestock. Their instruments were made out of stone, bones, and horns. Another ancient influential Chinese culture that came after the Yangshao Culture is the Longshan Culture (2400-1900 BC). This culture is located in China's Shandong Province. The people of this early culture learned to cultivate millet and rice. They also knew how to domesticate a variety of animals including dogs, cattle, sheep, chickens, and pigs. In creating their tools, they used

---

¹⁶ Joseph Miller, *The Emergence and Nature of Human History, Volume One* (Lulu.com, 2012), 373.

¹⁷ Craig G. Benjamin, *Foundations of Eastern Civilization*, Lectures 1-24 (Chantilly: The Teaching Company, 2013), 36.

¹⁸ Harold M. Tanner, *China: A History* (Cambridge: Hackett Publishing Co., 2009), 20.

stone, clams, jade, and bronze.[19]

Location of Yangshao Culture

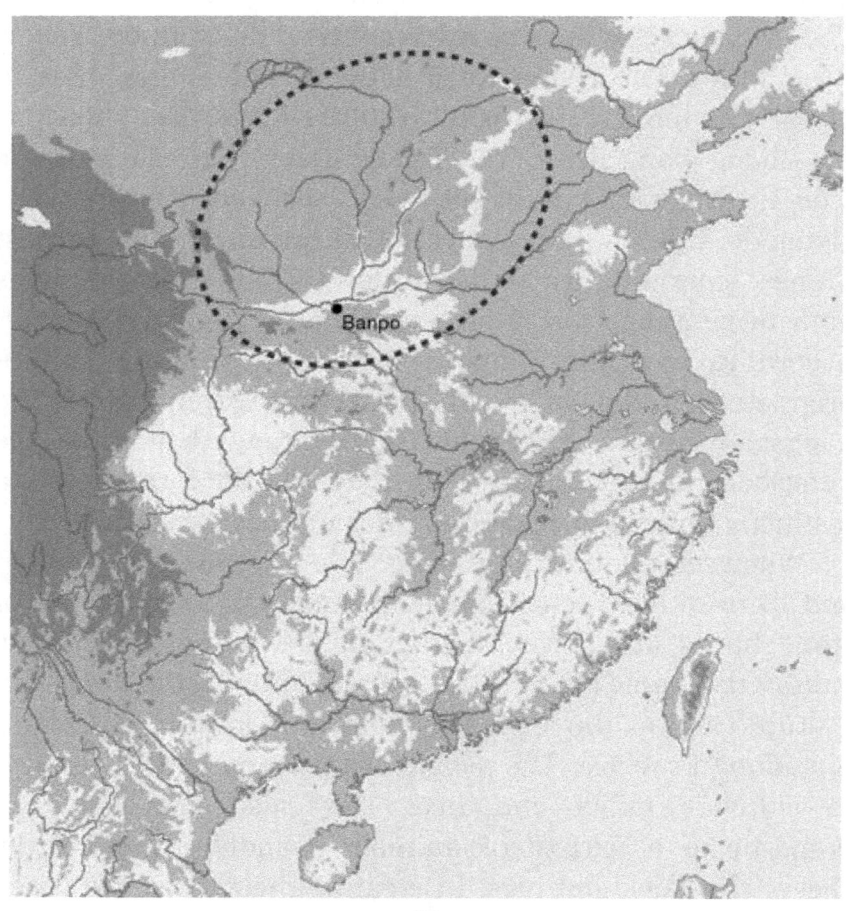

[20]

---

[19] The Editorial Committee of Chinese Civilization, *China: Five Thousand Years of History and Civilization* (Hong Kong: City University of Hong Kong Press, 2007), 9-11.

[20] Kanguole, "Area of the Yangshao culture (5000–3000 BC) in northern China, based on Liu Li and Chen Xingcan" (2012), *The Archaeology of China: From the Late Paleolithic to the Early Bronze Age*, Cambridge University Press, ISBN 978-0-521-64310-

Regional Cultures of the Yellow River Valley (3000s BC)

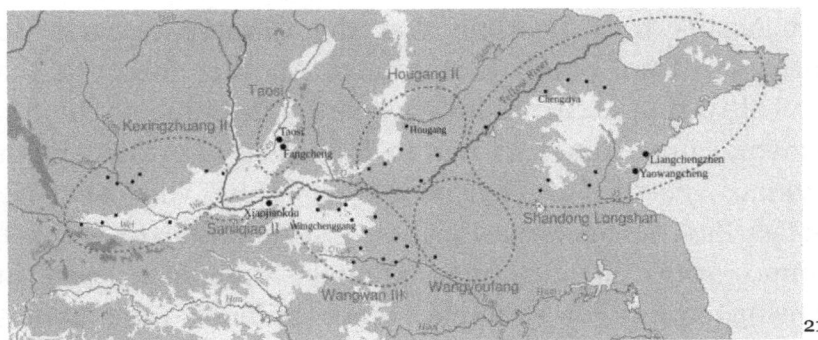

Evidence for early humans in South East Asia dates back to 40,000 years ago and possibly earlier. Bones and tools discovered on the Indonesia island of Java and on the multi-country island of Borneo, comprised of Indonesia, Malaysia, and Brunei, were dated to around this time.[22] Prehistoric rock art, such as in Thailand, has also given archaeologists data to determine the nature of daily human life in ancient East Asia. Some of the scenes from rock art indicate how the East Asian people gradually shifted away from hunting and gathering to a life of greater stability by farming.[23]

Since the warm climate of South East Asia is conducive to growing crops, South East Asia may have been one of the first places where early humans began to farm. This occurred during the 8000s BC. Archaeologists base this claim on their

---

8, p170," Map, https://commons.wikimedia.org/wiki/File:Yangshao_map.svg, (accessed October 27, 2015).

[21] Kanguole, "Regional cultures and local centers of the middle and lower Yellow River valley in the late 3rd millennium BC," map, https://www.commons.wikimedia.org/wiki/File:Longshan_cultures_and_centres.svg, (accessed October 28, 2015).

[22] Craig Lockard, *Southeast Asia in World History*, (Oxford: Oxford University Press, 2009), 5.

[23] Lockard, 8.

discoveries of various plant seeds. There is also some evidence that rice was first cultivated by humans in Southeast Asia.[24] It is possible that the Chinese learned rice cultivation from South East Asians. Another theory is that rice cultivation occurred independently in China.[25] The fundamental importance of rice in East Asia is evident in the standard greeting of Thai people of, "Have you eaten rice yet?"[26] East Asian domestication of animals dates back to around 3000 BC. In time, animals were also used for growing crops. For example, water buffalos were domesticated to plow fields in wet-rice farming.[27]

Water Buffalo Ploughing in Indonesia

[28]

---

[24] Lockard, 7.

[25] Patricia Ebrey, Anne Walthall, and James Palais, *East Asia: A Cultural, Social, and Political History* (Belmont: Wadsworth, 2009), 3.

[26] "Thai Food," Thailand Life, http://thailandlife.com/thai-food/index.php, (accessed October 28, 2015); Andrea Eisinberg, "Have You Eaten Rice Yet?" San Diego Reader, http://www.sandiegoreader.com/news/2012/aug/24/travel-thailand-have-you-eaten-rice-yet/ (accessed October 28, 2015).

[27] Lockard, 8.

[28] Udeyismail, "Water buffalo ploughing rice fields in Padang, West Sumatra, Indonesia," Photograph, https://upload.

Quiz 1

1-3. Explain how the term Asia originated. Include in your answer the following terms, ancient Europeans, *occidentem*, and *orientem*.

4-5. Identify the following regions: East Asia and South East Asia.

4.	5.
China, Taiwan, Japan, Mongolia, North Korea and South Korea	Vietnam, Cambodia, Brunei, Indonesia, Laos, Malaysia, Myanmar (also known as Burma), Philippines, Singapore, Thailand, and East Timor

6-8. With respect to water, distinguish in two ways the geography of East Asia from South East Asia. In addition, give an explanation of how the geography of these two

---

wikimedia.org/wikipedia/commons/5/52/Water_Buffalo_ploughing.jpg, (accessed October 28, 2015).

regions unites each one and distinguishes each one from one another.

    6.

    7.

    8.

9-10. To what period of time does pre-history refer, and where did pre-history first end?

    9.

    10.

11. In what region did the ancient Yangshao and Longshan cultures develop? (In answering this question, you need only identify the body of water around which the cultures grew.)

12-13. What artifacts did archaeologists use as data to determine daily human life of ancient East Asia? Name at least two.

    12.

    13.

    14. Why is rice so fundamental to East Asian culture? If you wish, and you have the acquired knowledge, you may answer this question from your own experience.

Chapter 2: East Asian Bronze Age

Introduction

The pre-historical Stone Age was followed by an age named the Bronze Age due to the use of bronze by early humans. It was during the Bronze Age that the first Asian writing was invented and then used to record history. The earliest archaeological evidence of bronze being used in China dates back to the Erlitou culture (c. 2100-1800 BC) of the Xia dynasty (c. 2070-c. 1600 BC).

The Xia dynasty, named after the Xia family who ruled in succession over China, is referred to in the ancient Chinese historical chronicle called the *Bamboo Annals*, and in the *Records of the Grand Historian* (100s BC) by Sima Qian.[29] Written records from the Xia dynasty do not exist. The earliest writing on Chinese history date to the dynasty that came immediately after the Xia dynasty, the Shang dynasty (1600-1046 BC). Writings from this time have been discovered on bones that are referred to as the oracle bones. The Shang people continued to master the use of bronze. South East Asian knowledge of working with bronze,

---

[29] Craig G. Benjamin, *Foundations of Eastern Civilization*, Lectures 1-24 (Chantilly: The Great Courses, 2013), 54-55.

speculate historians, probably originated from China.³⁰

Xia Dynasty

Whether the Xia dynasty (c.2070-c.1600 BC) actually existed is debated among historians since no contemporary documentary evidence has been discovered that dates back to the Xia dynasty. Nonetheless, there are references to the Xia dynasty in various literature written significantly after the Xia dynasty reputedly ended and was replaced by the Shang dynasty. One ancient text in which the Xia dynasty is referred to is the *Bamboo Annals*. The *Bamboo Annals*, also known as the *Jizhong Annals*, records ancient Chinese history in a chronological order. It was written around 300 BC on slips of bamboo. These slips have not survived the passage of time. All we currently have is a 16th century AD copied version of the text.³¹

Another early literary reference to the Xia dynasty is found in the *Records of the Grand Historian* by Sima Qian. Sima Qian (c. 145 -90 BC), also known as Zichang, was born in Xiayang of the Shannxi Chinese province. In 113 BC, he followed in his father's footsteps by inheriting the post of Grand Historian for Emperor Wu. A few years earlier, he had promised his dying father that he would write a history of China. He began chronicling China's history as the imperial Grand Historian. In 98 BC, his work was abruptly interrupted when he publicly insulted the Emperor by defending, in front of Emperor Wu, the Chinese general Li

---

³⁰ Craig Lockard, *Southeast Asia in World History*, (Oxford: Oxford University Press, 2009), 10.

³¹ "Bamboo Annals," Sourced from World Heritage Encyclopedia™ licensed under CC BY-SA 3.0, Project Gutenberg, http://self.gutenberg.org/articles/Bamboo_Annals (accessed November 3, 2015).

Ling who had been defeated in battle. In retaliation, the Emperor had Sima Qian imprisoned and castrated. Once Sima Qian was released from prison, he persevered in his promise to his father and completed the monumental work on ancient Chinese history called *The Records of the Grand Historian*.

The Records of the Grand Historian is divided into one hundred and thirty chapters. In all, it is over 500,000 words (Chinese characters) long. Sima Qian begins with a Chinese emperor called the Yellow Emperor who is reputed to have lived around 2500 BC. The records end with Sima Qian's own time of the Han Dynasty ruled by Emperor Wu.[32] In the excerpt below, Sima Qian refers to China's first dynasty, the Xia dynasty. The excerpt ends with the Han dynasty, under whose rule he lived. Notice his explanation for why a dynasty is replaced by another. According to Sima Qian, when rulers of a dynasty lose their virtue, the Gods of heaven will replace them with a more virtuous ruling family. This theory is called the Mandate of Heaven.

According to a Catholic understanding since God is all powerful he allows evil in the world, including permitting non-virtuous political regimes to exist, in order to draw forth a greater good that would not exist if God did not allow the regime to rule. As explained by Bishop Barron, with reference to St. Thomas Aquinas, without God's allowing for the cruelty and vices of tyrants there would be no virtue of the martyrs. God does not promise to deliver us from evil regimes, but he does assure us that he will be with us until the end of time as one who became one of us and willingly

---

[32] The Editorial Committee of Chinese Civilization, *China: Five Thousand Years of History and Civilization* (Hong Kong: City University of Hong Kong Press, 2007), 300-301.

suffered with us.[33] (Matthew 28:20)

Records of the Grand Historian

The government of the Xia dynasty was marked by good faith, which in time deteriorated until mean men had turned it into rusticity. Therefore, the men of Shang who succeeded to the Xia reformed this defect through the virtue of piety. But piety degenerated until mean men had made it a superstitious concern for the spirits. Therefore, the men of Zhou who followed corrected this fault through refinement and order. But refinement again deteriorated until it became in the hands of the mean a mere hollow show. Therefore, what was needed to reform this hollow show was a return to good faith, for the way of the Three Dynasties of old is like a cycle which, when it ends, must begin over again. It is obvious that in the late Zhou and Qin times the earlier refinement and order had deteriorated. But the government of Qin failed to correct this fault, instead adding its own harsh punishments and laws. Was this not a grave error? Thus when the Han rose to power it took over the faults of its predecessors and worked to change and reform them, causing men to be unflagging in their efforts and following the order properly ordained by Heaven. It held its court in the tenth month, and its vestments and carriage tops were

---

[33] Robert Barron, *The Mystery of God: Who God is and Why He Matters*, DVDs, (Word on Fire, 2015); cf. Thomas Aquinas, "Summa Theologica," I, q. 22, art. 2, New Advent, http://www.newadvent.org/summa/1022.htm, (accessed October 3, 2015).

yellow, with plumes on the left sides of the carriages.34

In 1959, archaeologists working in China uncovered an ancient city called Erlitou. According to radiocarbon dating, the city dates back to 2100-1800 years BC. This situates the people or Erlitou squarely within the Xia dynasty. It has been proposed that Erlitou was the capital city of the Xia dynasty. This, though, has not been sufficiently determined. Artifacts belonging to this early people indicate that the people had learned how to make bronze into vessels and into other objects.35 Bronze is made by smelting copper and another metal or metals, which usually includes tin, in order to create bronze. Bronze is more durable than copper alone.

Shang Dynasty

The Shang people demonstrated great mastery in their use of bronze. Many bronze artifacts from the Shang dynasty have been discovered along with other objects of historical interest. For example, in 1976 Chinese archaeologists unearthed the tomb of Lady Hao, which contained many items of the Shang people. This finding was remarkable since the tomb was intact and had not been robbed by grave diggers. Lady Hao may have been one of the wives of Emperor Wu Ding (reigned c. 1250-1192) BC. The reason why this theory is proposed is because of what was discovered in her tomb including, but not limited to, oracle bones, human skeletons, bronze objects, jade objects, stone sculptures, and hairpins.36

---

34 Sima Qian, *Records of the Grand Historian: Han dynasty*, Volume I, Revised Edition, trans. Burton Watson (New York: Columbia University Press, 1993), 85-86.
35 Benjamin, 54-55.
36 Benjamin, 73-74.

The bones referred to above as oracle bones in Lady Hao's tomb were also discovered in many other places. During the 1800s, these bones were superstitiously seen as magical bones of dragons that when ground up could heal a person who digested them. This practice was discouraged when scholars noticed ancient characters etched into the bones. The translations of this system of writing have provided much information about the Shang people.[37] Below is one such bone.

Oracle Bone

38

The human remains unearthed from Lady Hao's tomb consisted of 16 men, women, and children who had been

---

[37] Patricia Ebrey, Anne Walthall, and James Palais, *East Asia: A Cultural, Social, and Political History* (Belmont: Wadsworth, 2009), 12.

[38] BabelStone, "Oracle bone from the reign of King Wu Ding (late Shang dynasty)," photograph, http://www.commons.wikimedia.org/wiki/File%3AShang_dynasty_inscribed_scapula.jpg, (accessed June 7, 2015).

sacrificed.[39] Human sacrifices during the Shang dynasty were discovered in other sites as well. Those chosen as sacrificial victims were killed in a variety of ways including beating, beheading, and chopping to death.[40] The oracle bones have given scholars data that explain these horrific practices. Humans were ritually sacrificed to appease the Gods, especially the main God worshiped by the Shang kings, called Shangdi. The Shang dynasty claimed that Shangdi lived in a heavenly city named Shang. When members of the Shang dynasty died, they supposedly joined Shangdi in his heavenly realm. Worship of Shangdi, and lesser gods, therefore, entailed worshipping the ancestors of the Shang. This enforced worship of the Shangdi, minor Gods, and the ancestors of the Shang dynasty greatly helped to form a ritual that is prevalent throughout Asia: ancestor worship.[41]

Etchings on the oracle bones indicate that the Shang king consulted an oracle before choosing a date for ritualistic sacrifices and ancestor worship. The oracle bones also record the king's consulting oracles on more mundane matters including marriage, when to hunt, who to appoint, and who to dismiss. In total 155,000 oracle bone inscriptions with similar information have been studied. Almost every oracle bone has been dated to the Shang era.[42] The great value Shang kings placed on divination was also an influential historical factor for the current widespread Asian practice of fortune telling.

The two Shang practices of ancestor worship and

---

[39] Benjamin, 74.

[40] Benjamin, 67.

[41] Benjamin, 58-63; Alvyn Austin, *China's Millions* (Grand Rapids: Wm. B. Eerdmans, 2007), 155-156.

[42] Endymion Porter Wilkinson, *Chinese History: A Manual*, Revised and Enlarged (Cambridge: Harvard University Press, 2000), 390-395.

divination are, asserts Craig G. Benjamin, "foundational ritual practices of East Asian culture."[43] The Shang dynasty, Benjamin explains, "exerted tremendous influence on the emerging concepts of Eastern Civilization. I say 'Eastern' rather than 'Chinese' here because...Chinese culture came to exert an enormous degree of influence over all the other states and civilizations of East and Southeast Asia, including obviously those in Korea, Japan, and Vietnam."[44]

After Asia was evangelized by Christian missionaries, ancestor worship was modified by Catholics. Instead of worshipping ancestors, which is a violation of the First Commandment since worship is due to God alone, Asian Catholics began venerating their ancestors by remembering them, praying for them, and, at times, praying to them as people ask the living to pray to God for them.

South East Asian Bronze Age

Around 2000 BC, South East Asia began making bronze instruments. Some scholars claim that the South East Asians learned bronze working from China.[45] Another possibility is that South East Asians learned bronze making independently of China.[46] Archaeologists have discovered cooking utensils, weapons and other simple bronze items from this early East Asian period. About 1500 BC, the people of Northeast Thailand had mastered fine bronze making.[47] Below, is an example of fine bronze making from Vietnam's Bronze Age. The bronze drum comes from Song Da Vietnam and was

---

[43] Benjamin, 68.

[44] Benjamin, 68.

[45] Lockard, 10.

[46] Charles Higham, *The Bronze Age of Southeast Asia* (Cambridge: Cambridge University Press, 1996), 5, 13.

[47] Lockard, 10.

made during the 1000s BC.

Quiz 2

1. In what age was Asian writing first invented?

2-8. What is a dynasty? Why is there debate on whether the Xia Dynasty or the Shang Dynasty was China's first dynasty? In answering this question, include the following: archaeological evidence, radio carbon dating, contemporary documentary evidence, historical chronicle, and the *Records of the Grand Historian*.

2.

3.

---

[48] Author not specified, "Dong Son II Culture. Mid 1st Millenium BCE. Bronze," photograph, https://www.commons.wikimedia.org/wiki/File%3ATambour-song-da2.jpg (accessed November 10, 2015).

4-8.

9-13. Who was Sima Qian? What was his explanation for the fall of one Chinese dynasty and the rise of another? How does a Catholic explanation for the fall and rise of a political regime differ from Sima Qian's? Include in your answer the following: providence, martyrs, and tyrants.

9.

10.

11-13.

14. What are the oracle bones?

15-16. Distinguish between ancestor worship of the Shang Dynasty and ancestor veneration as practiced by Catholics.

Chapter 3: East Asian Iron Age

Introduction

China's Shang dynasty was replaced by the Zhou dynasty (c. 1045-256 BC). To justify the regime change, the Zhou people claimed they had received a Mandate from Heaven. During the reign of the Zhou Dynasty the Chinese learned how to use iron. Due to certain advantages that iron has over bronze, iron increasingly became preferred to bronze. In studying the Iron Age, we will focus our attention on China's Western Zhou period (1045-770 BC) and on its Eastern Zhou period (770-221 AD). Confucianism and Legalism developed during the Zhou dynasty. These two philosophies have profoundly influenced not only China, out of which they arose, but all of East Asia. The philosophy that has been more influential is undoubtedly Confucianism, especially in South Eastern lands (Korea and Vietnam) that were once ruled by China's Han dynasty (206 BC-220 AD), a dynasty that adopted Confucianism as its philosophy.

Zhou Dynasty

The Zhou dynasty was divided into two phases corresponding to different regions in China where the Zhou ruled, west and east. The Western Zhou dynasty lived in Western China from about 1045-770 BC. The Western Zhou dynasty came to an end when the Zhou King You banished his wife to marry his concubine. His wife complained to her father who was a powerful ruler in Eastern China. Her father became enraged and set out to punish King You. As a result, in 770 BC the Western Zhou dynasty fell and was replaced by an Eastern Zhou dynasty with an eastern capital city.[49] The Eastern Zhou dynasty lasted from around 770 to 256 BC. The Eastern Zhou dynasty is in turn divided into two sub-periods: The Spring and Autumn Period (722-481 BC) and The Warring States Period (480-256 BC).

Five influential literary works that in the Han dynasty (206 BC-220 AD) were considered the Five Classics of Confucianism all were written during the Zhou Dynasty. They include the Book of Changes (*Yijing*), Book of Documents (*Shujing*), Book of Rites (*Liji*), Book of Odes (*Shijing*), and Spring and Autumn annals (*Chun Qiu*).[50] A history of the Zhou dynasty is contained in the collection of historical documents called the *Book of Documents*. This work explicitly refers to the Mandate of Heaven that provides justification for the rise of the Zhou people and the fall of the Shang dynasty. Below is an excerpt from the *Book of Documents* on the Mandate of Heaven. The "Yin Dynasty" that the excerpt refers to is the Shang dynasty. According to the Mandate of Heaven, dynasties, such as the Xia and Shang, fell because they fell out of favor with the Gods who disapproved of the non-virtuous practices of the dynastic leaders.

In the previous chapter you were introduced to the Mandate of Heaven by way of Sima Qian's *The Records of*

---

[49] Craig G. Benjamin, *Foundations of Eastern Civilization*, Lectures 1-24 (Chantilly: The Great Courses, 2013), 92-98.

[50] Dorothy Perkins, *Encyclopedia of China: History and Culture* (London: Routledge, 1999), 160.

the Grand Historian. As Catholics we believe that the virtuous are not necessarily blessed in this life but will be blessed in the life to come. Simply because someone prospers in this life does not mean that God favors that way of life, as the Mandate of Heaven seems to indicate. That God allows in this present life the wicked to prosper and the virtuous to suffer causes us to resonate with Job's cry, "Why do the wicked live on, reach old age, and grow mighty in power?" (Job 21:7 NRSV) Working subtly through history (Wisdom 8:1), God, in preparation for the final consummation of the world when Christ will come to judge the living and dead, "ordereth all things sweetly." (Wisdom 8:1 DRA)

Mandate from Heaven

~ The Announcement of the Duke of Shao ~

5 ('When the work was drawing to a completion), the Grand-Guardian went out with the hereditary princes of the various states to bring their offerings (for the king); and when he entered again, he gave them to the duke of Zhou, saying, 'With my hands to my head and my head to the ground, I present these to his Majesty and your Grace. Announcements for the information of the multitudes of Yin [Shang] must come from you, with whom is the management of affairs.' 'Oh! God (dwelling in) the great heavens has changed his decree respecting his great son and the great dynasty of Yin [Shang]. Our king has received that decree. Unbounded is the happiness connected with it, and unbounded is the anxiety: Oh! how can he be other than reverent?

6. When Heaven rejected and made an end of the decree in favor of the great dynasty of Yin [Shang], there were

many of its former wise kings in heaven. The king, however, who had succeeded to them, the last of his race, from the time of his entering into their appointment, proceeded in such a way as at last to keep the wise in obscurity and the vicious in office. The poor people in such a case, carrying their children and leading their wives, made their moan to Heaven. They even fled away, but were apprehended again. Oh! Heaven had compassion on the people of the four quarters; its favoring decree lighted on our earnest (founders). Let the king sedulously cultivate the virtue of reverence.

7. Examining the men of antiquity, there was the (founder of the) Xia dynasty. Heaven guided (his mind), allowed his descendants (to succeed him), and protected them. He acquainted himself with Heaven, and was obedient to it. But in process of time the decree in his favor fell to the ground. So also is it now when we examine the case of Yin [Shang]. There was the same guiding (of its founder), who corrected (the errors of Xia), and (whose descendants) enjoyed the protection (of Heaven). He (also) acquainted himself with Heaven, and was obedient to it. But now the decree in favor of him has fallen to the ground. Our king has' now come to the throne in his youth; let him not slight the aged and experienced, for it may be said of them that they have studied the virtuous conduct of the ancients, and have matured their counsels in the sight of Heaven.

...

9. 'We should by all means survey the dynasties of Xia and Yin [Shang]. I do not presume to know and say, "The dynasty of Xia was to enjoy the favoring decree of Heaven just for (so many) years," nor do I presume to know and say, "It could not continue longer." The fact simply was,

that, for want of the virtue of reverence, the decree in its favor prematurely fell to the ground. (Similarly), I do not presume to know and say, "The dynasty of Yin [Shang] was to enjoy the favoring decree of Heaven just for (so many) years," nor do I presume to know and say, "It could not continue longer." The fact simply was, that, for want of the virtue of reverence, the decree in its favor fell prematurely to the ground. The king has now inherited the decree - the same decree, I consider, which belonged to those two dynasties. Let him seek to inherit (the virtues of) their meritorious (sovereigns).

...

11. 'In the position of king, let him not, because of the excesses of the people in violation of the laws, presume also to rule by the violent infliction of death; when the people are regulated gently, the merit (of government) is seen. It is for him who is in the position of king to overtop all with his virtue. In this case the people will imitate him throughout the kingdom, and he will become still more illustrious. Let the king and his ministers labor with a mutual sympathy, saying, "We have received the decree of Heaven, and it shall be great as the long-continued years of Xia; yea, it shall not fail of the long-continued years of Yin." I wish the king, through (the attachment of) the lower people, to receive the long-abiding decree of Heaven.'

12. (The duke of Shao) then did obeisance with his hands to his head and his head to the ground, and said, 'I, a small minister, presume, with the king's (heretofore) hostile people and all their officers, and with his (loyal) friendly people, to maintain and receive his majesty's dread command and brilliant virtue. That the king should finally obtain the decree all-complete, and that he should

become illustrious' - this I do not presume to labor for. I only bring respectfully these offerings to present to his majesty, to be used in his prayers to Heaven for its long-abiding decree.'[51]

Along with the *Book of Documents*, the other four Confucian classics have, explains Michael Nylan, "as a whole occupied in East Asia a position roughly analogous to that of the Bible in the West."[52] A main reason why these classics had, and still have, such a profound influence is that they were used for centuries to test candidates who wished to work in the Chinese government. This Confucian based civil service exam was officially mandated by Emperor Wu (r. 140-86 BC) of the Han dynasty. Not until the founding of the Republic of China in 1912 and end of China's last dynasty, was Confucianism decoupled from the Chinese government.[53]

Prior to Emperor Wu and his Han dynasty, Confucianism was not the dominant philosophy, Legalism was. Legalism, interestingly as we will see, developed out of the teachings of Xunzi, a disciple of Confucius (c. 551-479 BC). Confucius, whom Xunzi identified as his intellectual master, was born in the regional state of Lu during the first sub-period of the Eastern Zhou dynasty called the Spring and Autumn period. During the Spring and Autumn period powerful families were jostling for power. Feuds between these families were common place. In the midst of these

---

[51] "Announcement of the Duke of Shao," trans. James Legge, Chinese Text Project, http://ctext.org/shang-shu/announcement-of-the-duke-of-shao, (accessed November 13, 2015).

[52] Michael Nylan, *The Five "Confucian" Classics* (New Haven: Yale University Press, 2001), 2

[53] Craig G. Benjamin, *Foundations of Eastern Civilization*, Lectures 1-24 (Chantilly: The Great Courses, 2013), 204-207.

tense times, Confucius was able to obtain a minor administrative position in the state government. Eventually, he held the position of minister of crime in his state of Lu. In 497 BC, at age fifty-four, he resigned from his office.[54] Confucius drew to himself students who collected and compiled his oral teachings into the *Analects*. The *Analects* teach that a well-ordered society needs to be hierarchically based and led by virtuous people. Main virtues that Confucius encourages in the *Analects* are filial piety, scholarship, and active civic duty. Confucian virtues related to these principal ones are loyalty, honesty, reverence, respect, benevolence, and ritual decorum.[55]

When the Spring and Autumn Period ended and was replaced by the chaotic Warring States Period, the rulers and the people did not look to Confucianism, which insisted rulers needed to be virtuous, but rather to the legalists who did not assert this principle. According to the legalists, what is important is not the virtue of a leader but rather the upholding of law. The ascendancy of Legalism was prepared by the Confucian Xunzi.

Xunzi and Mencius

One way to understand Xunzi (c. 300-210 BC) with clarity is to contrast him with a contemporary Confucian scholar named Mencius (327-289 BC). In accordance with Confucian thought, both Xunzi and Mencius valued the

---

[54] Annping Chin, *Confucius: A Life of Thought and Politics* (New Haven: Yale University Press, 2008), 2-3, 13, 23.

[55] Patricia Ebrey, Anne Walthall, and James Palais, *East Asia: A Cultural, Social, and Political History* (Belmont: Wadsworth, 2009), 26.

virtues of filial piety, education, and active civic duty.[56] They differed in how they understood how human beings become virtuous. Mencius held that virtue comes naturally to human beings. He asserted, "The goodness of human nature is like the downward course of water. There is no human being lacking in the tendency to do good, just as there is no water lacking in the tendency to flow downward."[57] In contrast, Xunzi argued that human beings are naturally vicious and self-centered. According to him, "human nature is evil and that any good in humans is acquired by conscious exertion."[58] Virtue, therefore, needs to be taught and regulated by laws that are to be enforced in a rigorous manner; otherwise, human beings will easily return to their more natural, vicious, self-centered tendencies.[59]

Xunzi and Mencius lived during the time of The Warring States Period (480-256 BC), which was a period of a multicentric civil war between various Chinese states. During these turbulent times, where human life was killed so frequently, Xunzi's pessimistic concept of human nature made more sense to many than Mencius' positive explanation of human nature.[60] What particularly drew people to Xunzi's Confucianism was his belief that enforcing law will bring order. This led to the development of a school of Legalism, which rose to prominence when the Qin State

---

[56] Grant Hardy, *Great Minds of the Eastern Intellectual Tradition*, Lectures 1-18 (Chantilly: The Great Courses, 2011), 117-120.

[57] Mencius, *Mencius*, trans. Irene Bloom (New York: Columbia University Press, 2009), 121.

[58] Xunzi, *Xunzi: A Translation and Study of the Complete Works, Volume III, Books 17-32*, trans. John Knoblock (Stanford: Stanford University Press, 1994), 153.

[59] Xunzi, 157-158.

[60] Hardy, 130.

overthrew the last Zhou king and began its short-lived Qin Empire (221-206 BC).

Legalism

Two important legalists were the Lord Shang (d. 338 BC), who worked for the Qin State, and Han Feizi (d. 233 BC). In the *Book of Lord Shang*, that Lord Shang reputedly wrote, "virtue has its origin in punishment."[61] To bring about the maximum amount of virtue, Lord Shang advocated harsh penalties and light rewards.[62] He justified this practice by explaining, "For the more punishments there are, the more valued are rewards, and the fewer rewards there are, the more heed is paid to punishments, by virtue of the fact that people have desires and dislikes."[63] Han Feizi, who had been a student of Xunzi, explicitly rejected Confucius and his emphasis on virtue. Instead, he sided with Lord Shang's legalist views. According to Han Feizi, an effective ruler is to punish with severity, take credit for success, blame his subordinates for failures, and never "reveal his nature" to his subordinates so as to be better able to manipulate them.[64]

Legalism and Warfare

One famous work that represents the school of Legalism with its emphasis on law harshly laid down by cunning,

---

[61] Yang Shang, "The Book of Lord Shang, trans. Jan Julius Lodewijk" Elimination of Strength, no. 4, Chinese Text Project, http://ctext.org/shang-jun-shu/order-to-cultivate-waste-lands, (accessed August 3, 2015).

[62] Shang, "The Book of Lord Shang."

[63] Shang, "The Book of Lord Shang."

[64] Han Feizi, *Han Feizi: Basic Writings*, trans. Burton Watson (New York: Columbia University Press, 2003), 36; Hardy, 142.

deceitful rulers is *The Art of War* by Sun Tzu. This work was likely written around the 4th century BC during the Warring States Era. It has been studied with great care by military leaders, politicians, and businessmen.[65] Below are a few excerpts from *The Art of War*. Read them critically in light of the Catholic faith.

~ *The Art of War* by Sun Tzu ~

I. Laying Plans

1. Sun Tzu said: The art of war is of vital importance to the State.
...
18. All warfare is based on deception.
19. Hence, when able to attack, we must seem unable; when using our forces, we must seem inactive; when we are near, we must make the enemy believe we are far away; when far away, we must make him believe we are near.
20. Hold out baits to entice the enemy. Feign disorder, and crush him.
21. If he is secure at all points, be prepared for him. If he is in superior strength, evade him.
22. If your opponent is of choleric temper, seek to irritate him. Pretend to be weak, that he may grow arrogant.
23. If he is taking his ease, give him no rest. If his forces are united, separate them.
24. Attack him where he is unprepared, appear where you are not expected.
...

---

[65] Hardy, 138.

III. Attack by Stratagem

1. Sun Tzu said: In the practical art of war, the best thing of all is to take the enemy's country whole and intact; to shatter and destroy it is not so good. So, too, it is better to recapture an army entire than to destroy it, to capture a regiment, a detachment or a company entire than to destroy them.

2. Hence to fight and conquer in all your battles is not supreme excellence; supreme excellence consists in breaking the enemy's resistance without fighting.

...

IV. Tactical Dispositions

1. Sun Tzu said: The good fighters of old first put themselves beyond the possibility of defeat, and then waited for an opportunity of defeating the enemy.

...

VI. Weak Points and Strong

...

30. So in war, the way is to avoid what is strong and to strike at what is weak.

...

32. Therefore, just as water retains no constant shape, so in warfare there are no constant conditions.

33. He who can modify his tactics in relation to his opponent and thereby succeed in winning, may be called a heaven-born captain.

...

VII. Maneuvering

...

15. In war, practice dissimulation, and you will succeed.

...

XIII. The Use of Spies

...

7. Hence the use of spies, of whom there are five classes: (1) Local spies; (2) inward spies; (3) converted spies; (4) doomed spies; (5) surviving spies.

8. When these five kinds of spy are all at work, none can discover the secret system. This is called "divine manipulation of the threads." It is the sovereign's most precious faculty.

9. Having local spies means employing the services of the inhabitants of a district.

10. Having inward spies, making use of officials of the enemy.

11. Having converted spies, getting hold of the enemy's spies and using them for our own purposes.

12. Having doomed spies, doing certain things openly for purposes of deception, and allowing our spies to know of them and report them to the enemy.

13. Surviving spies, finally, are those who bring back news from the enemy's camp.

...

18. Be subtle! be subtle! and use your spies for every kind of business.

...

23. It is owing to his information, again, that we can cause the doomed spy to carry false tidings to the enemy.

...

27. Hence it is only the enlightened ruler and the wise general who will use the highest intelligence of the army for purposes of spying and thereby they achieve great results. Spies are a most important element in water,

because on them depends an army's ability to move.[66]

A Catholic Response to Legalism

According to Catholicism, for a human action to be morally good, the moral object must be good, such as telling the truth. It is to be done in the right circumstances, for example revealing the truth to those who have the right to know the truth. It must also be done with good intentions, ultimately out of love of God and neighbor and not for self-glorification. As the *Catechism of the Catholic Church* succinctly states:

> A *morally good* act requires the goodness of the object, of the end, and of the circumstances together. An evil end corrupts the action, even if the object is good in itself (such as praying and fasting "in order to be seen by men"). The *object of the choice* can by itself vitiate an act in its entirety. There are some concrete acts—such as fornication—that it is always wrong to choose, because choosing them entails a disorder of the will, that is, a moral evil.[67]

In light of these three sources of morality, the Catholic philosopher Peter Kreeft explains what is wrong with Legalism. In so doing, he contrasts legalism with more modern trends of Relativism and Subjectivism. Legalism

---

[66] Sun Tzu, "The Art of War," trans. Lionel Giles, Internet Classics Archive, http://www.classics.mit.edu/Tzu/artwar.html, (accessed November 13, 2015).

[67] "Catechism of the Catholic Church, Second Edition," no. 1755, USCCB, http://www.usccb.org/beliefs-and-teachings/what-we-believe/catechism/catechism-of-the-catholic-church/epub/index.cfm#, (accessed November 15, 2015).

defines moral behavior by good actions while ignoring the importance of right intention and fitting circumstances. In contrast, Relativism only acknowledges fitting circumstances, and Subjectivism only focuses on right intention.[68] Kreeft writes:

> A human act must be whole to be good, as the human body must have a whole set of working organs to be healthy. Any one malfunctioning organ can kill you; thus defect in any one of the three dimensions of morality can make the act wrong. Or, to use another analogy for the same point, a moral act is like a work of art. If a piece of music is too loud, or too long, or too sweet, or too sour, it is defective. Or if a story has unbelievable characters, or theme, or plot, or style, it is a bad story even if its other dimensions are good. Everything counts.[69]

Quiz 3

1-6. Place the following dynasties in their proper chronological order. Eastern Zhou Dynasty, Western Zhou Dynasty, Shang Dynasty, Xia Dynasty, The Warring States Period, The Spring and Autumn Period.

2-5. Name and briefly define the two main philosophies, discussed in chapter three, that developed during the Zhou

---

[68] Peter Kreeft, *Practical Theology: Spiritual Direction from Saint Thomas Aquinas* (San Francisco: Ignatius Press, 2014), 85.
[69] Kreeft, 85.

dynasty and have influenced East Asia.

6-7. Compare and contrast the two philosophies referred to above.

7-8. Compare and contrast Xunzi and Mencius.

9-11. Critique legalism in light of the three moral sources referred to by the *Catechism of the Catholic Church*.

Chapter 4: Early Diversification of East Asian Civilization

Introduction

The previous chapter focused on early Chinese history, a period during which China became known as "the great cultural giant of East Asia." From that central point, Craig G. Benjamin explains, "Chinese culture came to exert an enormous degree of influence over the other states and civilizations of East and Southeast Asia."[70] This chapter will study how East Asian culture became diversified with distinct cultures. Before doing so, though, we will study China's great, long lasting Han dynasty (206 BC-220 AD) during which China exerted its imperial might over other cultures. The Han dynasty was divided into two periods: Western Han (206 BC-9 AD) and Eastern Han (25 AD-220 AD). These two periods of Han rule were divided by the brief rule of the Xin Dynasty (9-23 AD).[71]

---

[70] Craig G. Benjamin, *Foundations of Eastern Civilization*, Lectures 1-24 (Chantilly: The Great Courses, 2013), 68.

[71] Patricia Ebrey, Anne Walthall, and James Palais, *East Asia: A Cultural, Social, and Political History* (Belmont: Wadsworth, 2009), 41-43.

Han Dynasty

Below is a map of the Western Han Dynasty in 1 AD.

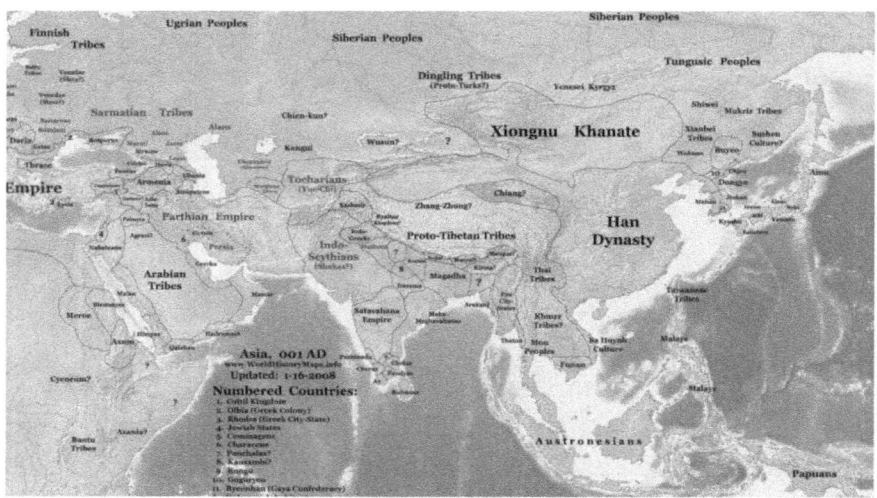

Emperor Wu of the Western Han Dynasty

Emperor Wu (r. 141-86 BC) was one of the most influential emperors of the Han dynasty. Under his rule, a Han-Confucian political-philosophical synthesis officially began. To promote Confucianism, he established an Imperial University dedicated to the training of governmental officials in Confucian thought. He also established a method for selecting officials according to the degree they manifested Confucian virtues. In subsequent dynasties, Confucian-based civil-service exams were established. Emperor Wu began a merit based system in which governmental officials needed

---

[72] Thomas A. Lessman, "Image was created by me (Thomas Lessman) based on map of Eastern Hemisphere in 001 AD," map, https://commons.wikimedia.org/wiki/File%3AAsia_001ad.jpg, (accessed November 22, 2015).

to prove their scholarship. Not only did Emperor Wu order his realm around Confucianism, but he also introduced the Han-Confucian synthesis into other cultures by expanding his vast empire into Eastern Central Asia and into Korea and Vietnam. In order to manage his vast empire and to raise funds, he established governmental monopolies of alcohol, salt and iron production.[73] Much of what we know about Emperor Wu's achievements comes from the Han imperial court historian Sima Qian in his *Records of the Grand Historian*.[74]

Wang Mang of the Xin Dynasty

The Han dynasty was briefly interrupted by a governmental official named Wang Mang who overthrew the Han and established himself as Emperor of a new dynasty called the Xin Dynasty, which in English means New Dynasty. The Xin Dynasty only lasted from 9-23 AD. It was replaced by the Eastern Han Dynasty, which established its capital in Eastern China, hence the name. Prior to Wang Mang's coup, the Han Dynasty had entered into a phase of corruption where the peasants were at the verge of attempting to overthrow their wealthy landlords. The peasants were in a position to achieve this goal since central authority had been greatly weakened by aristocratic families. These royal families had weakened central authority by

---

[73] Ebrey, Walthall, and Palais, 43; Mark Edward Lewis, *The Early Chinese Empires: Qin and Han* (Cambridge: Harvard University Press, 2007), 20; Grant Hardy, and Anne Behnke Kinney, *The Establishment of the Han Empire and Imperial China* (Westport: Greenwood Press, 2005), 26.

[74] Burton Watson, *Records of the Grand historian: Han Dynasty II*, trans. Burton Watson (New York: Columbia University Press, 1993), xiii.

placing on the throne very young boys who were easily manipulated.

Pingdi (9 BC – 6 AD) was only eight years old when he became emperor. Pingdi's successor, Ruzi, was only two years old when he gained the throne. During Ruzi's rule, Wang Mang acted as the actual emperor. When Emperor Ruzi reached the age of about four years old, Wang Mang declared himself the emperor and appealed to the Mandate of Heaven to justify the regime change. When Wang Mang took the throne, he tried to restore justice by taking land away from wealthy landlords and claiming them as "the king's fields."[75] In other words, he nationalized land. Afterwards, land was redistributed in a manner that Wang Mang thought was just.[76] Wang Mang also nationalized gold. Not surprisingly, resentment began building up against Wang Mang. When the Yellow River flooded and millions of farmers were dislocated, the Han family seized this opportune moment and led a rebellion that ended with the Han back in power. They re-established their empire by shifting their capital eastwards, thereby beginning the Eastern Han Dynasty (25-220 AD).[77]

Ban Zhao of the Eastern Han Dynasty

Instead of focusing on the emperors of the Eastern Han Dynasty, who were not that notable, we will turn our attention to a famous woman from the Eastern Han Dynasty, Ban Zhao (45-116 AD). The emperors from this time were weak since they had capitulated much of their power to court

---

[75] Charles F.W. Higham, *Encyclopedia of Ancient Asian Civilizations* (New York: Facts on File, 2004), 368.
[76] Higham, 368.
[77] Ebrey, Walthall, and Palais, 43.

eunuchs, castrated men who served the emperor. These eunuchs eventually ruled behind the scene with the emperor ruling in name only. In contrast to the weak emperors of the Eastern Han Dynasty, Ban Zhao was a strong woman who became one of the most renowned of China's women scholars.[78] She married young at age fourteen, but her husband died soon after they were married. She exhibited her strength by refusing to remarry and choosing to devote her life to study.

Two of her works are the *Book of Han* and *Lessons for Women*. The *Book of Han*, a history on the Han dynasty, was begun by her father, continued by Ban Zhao's brother and completed by Ban Zhao. Her *Lessons for Women* contain advice for women. She argues that men and women both need to be educated. In her *Lessons for Women* she asserts, "[O]nly to teach men and not to teach women—is that not ignoring the essential relation between them? According to *The Record of Rites*, it is the rule to begin to teach children to read at the age of eight years, and by the age of fifteen years they ought then to be ready for cultural training. Only why should it not be (that girls' education as well as boys' be) according to this principle?"[79] This bold assertion of hers served as a source of inspiration for women of her time who would later seek to be educated. Below are a few other excerpts from her book.

---

[78] Ebrey, Walthall, and Palais, 44.
[79] Robin R. Wang, *Images of Women in Chinese Thought and Culture: Writings from the Pre-Qin through the Song Dynasty*, (Cambridge: Hackett Publishing Co., 2003), 178-179.

Fr. Peter Samuel Kucer, MSA

~ *Lessons for Women* ~
by Ban Zhao

I, the unworthy writer, am unsophisticated, unenlightened, and by nature unintelligent, but I am fortunate both to have received not a little favor from my scholarly father, and to have had a (cultured) mother and instructresses upon whom to rely for a literary education as well as for training in good manners. More than forty years have passed since at the age of fourteen I took up the dustpan and broom in the Ts'ao family. During this time with trembling heart I feared constantly that I might disgrace my parents, and that I might multiply difficulties for both the women and the men (of my husband's family). Day and night I was distressed in heart, (but) I labored without confessing weariness. Now and hereafter, however, I know how to escape (from such fears).

...I grieve that you, my daughters, just now at the age for marriage, have not at this time had gradual training and advice; that you still have not learned the proper customs for married women. I fear that by failure in good manners in other families you will humiliate both your ancestors and your clan. ... In order that you may have something wherewith to benefit your persons, I wish every one of you, my daughters, each to write out a copy for yourself.
...

Chapter One: Humility

On the third day after the birth of a girl the ancients observed three customs: (first) to place the baby below the bed; (second) to give her a potsherd with which to play; and (third) to announce her birth to her ancestors by an offering. Now to lay the baby below the bed plainly indicated that she is lowly and weak, and should regard it as her primary duty to humble herself before others. To give her potsherds with which to play indubitably signified that she should practice labor and consider it her primary duty to be industrious. To announce her birth before her ancestors clearly meant that she ought to esteem as her primary duty the continuation of the observance of worship in the home.

These three ancient customs epitomize a woman's ordinary way of life and the teachings of the traditional ceremonial rites and regulations. Let a woman modestly yield to others; let her respect others; let her put others first, herself last. Should she do something good, let her not mention it; should she do something bad, let her not deny it. Let her bear disgrace; let her even endure when others speak and do evil to her. Always let her seem to tremble and fear. (When a woman follows such maxims as these,) then she may be said to humble herself before others.

Let a woman retire late to bed, but rise early to duties; let her not dread tasks by day or by night. Let her not refuse to perform domestic duties whether easy or difficult. That which must be done, let her finish completely, tidily, and systematically...

Let a woman be correct in manner and upright in character in order to serve her husband. Let her live in purity and quietness (of spirit) and attend to her own affairs. Let her love not gossip and silly laughter. Let her cleanse and purify and arrange in order the wine and the food for the offerings to the ancestors. (When a woman observes such principles as these,) then she may be said to continue ancestral worship.

No woman who observes these three (fundamentals of life) has ever had a bad reputation or has fallen into disgrace. If a woman fails to observe them, how can her name be honored; how can she bring disgrace upon herself?

Chapter Two: Husband and Wife

The Way of husband and wife is intimately connected with *yin* and *yang*, and relates the individual to gods and ancestors. Truly it is the great principle of Heaven and Earth, and the great basis of human relationships. Therefore, *The Record of Rites* honors the union of man and woman, and in *The Book of Odes* the First Ode manifests the principle of marriage. For these reasons, the relationship cannot but be an important one.

If a husband be unworthy, then he possesses nothing by which to control his wife. If a wife be unworthy, then she possesses nothing with which to serve her husband. If a husband does not control his wife, then the rules of conduct manifesting his authority are abandoned and broken. If a wife does not serve her husband, then the proper relationship (between men and women) and the natural order of things are neglected and destroyed. As a matter of fact, the purpose of these two (the controlling of women by men, and the serving of men by women) is the same.

Now examine the gentlemen of the present age. They only

know that wives must be controlled, and that the husband's rules of conduct manifesting his authority must be established. They therefore teach their boys to read books and (study) histories. But they do not in the least understand that husbands and masters must (also) be served, and that the proper relationship and the rites should be maintained.[80]

As you read the excerpts compare and contrast St. Paul's (in Ephesians 5:21-33) advice to married couples with Ban Zhao's. One difference that clearly distinguishes Ban Zhao's advice from St. Paul's is how the two strive to motivate people to act properly. Ban Zhao urges a woman to behave in order to bring honor to herself and her family (both those who are deceased and those who are living). St. Paul, in contrast, urges his brethren "by the mercies of God, to present [their] bodies a living and holy sacrifice, acceptable to God, which is your spiritual service of worship." (Romans 12:1 NAB) In other words, St. Paul incorporates in his exhortations a vertical dimension to God that Ban Zhao's writings lacks. For this reason, when St. Paul refers to guilt, he is primarily describing a reality in which Christians have offended God who knows all our secrets. Ban Zhao, however, refers to guilt from the standpoint of a horizontal dimension in the sense of the shame a person will experience by what other human beings will think of actions that are not in accordance with proper etiquette.

Ephesians 5:21-33

Be subject to one another out of reverence for Christ. Wives, be subject to your husbands, as to the Lord. For

---

[80] Wang, 178-179.

the husband is the head of the wife as Christ is the head of the church, his body, and is himself its Savior. As the church is subject to Christ, so let wives also be subject in everything to their husbands. Husbands, love your wives, as Christ loved the church and gave himself up for her, that he might sanctify her, having cleansed her by the washing of water with the word, that he might present the church to himself in splendor, without spot or wrinkle or any such thing, that she might be holy and without blemish. Even so husbands should love their wives as their own bodies. He who loves his wife loves himself. For no man ever hates his own flesh, but nourishes and cherishes it, as Christ does the church, because we are members of his body. "For this reason a man shall leave his father and mother and be joined to his wife, and the two shall become one flesh." This is a great mystery, and I mean in reference to Christ and the church; however, let each one of you love his wife as himself, and let the wife see that she respects her husband.

Diversification of East Asian Cultures

From the Han Dynasty to around 600 AD, South East Asian cultures were significantly influenced by Chinese and Indian culture. This was directly the case in northern Vietnam which was ruled by the Chinese during the Han dynasty. The Chinese spread their influence in other South East Cultures by way of trade. India also gained influence over South East cultures by way of trade routes and through Indian priests who travelled to South East Asia. The South East regions currently known as Cambodia, Thailand, Vietnam, Burma, and the Malay archipelago (which includes Brunei, Indonesia, Malaysia, Singapore and Southern Thailand) established states strongly influenced by Hindu and Buddhist beliefs.[81] The Chinese and Indian influence over early South East Asia should not be interpreted as if Chinese and Indian cultures were responsible for the formation of early South East Asian cultures. Rather, they were important factors that helped to shape these cultures that gradually emerged.[82]

Funan

The first South East Asian Empire was Funan (c. 150-550). The term Funan comes from China and may not have been how the people of the empire referred to themselves.[83] According to tradition, a Brahman Indian named Kaundinya married a local tribal princess from southeastern Cambodia and then established the Funan kingdom. In time, Funan developed into an empire that included all of Cambodia and reached even into the Malay Peninsula. In this empire, Buddhism and Hinduism were both practiced.[84] Below is a stele found in Vietnam that dates back to the kingdom of Funan. The Sanskrit writing describes a donation given in honor to the Hindu God Vishnu by Prince Gunavarman.

---

[81] Milton W. Meyer, *Asia: A Concise History* (Lanham: Rowman & Littlefield Publishers, 1997), 61-62.

[82] M.C. Ricklefs, Bruce Lockhart, Albert Lau, Portia Reyes, and Maitrii Aung-Thwin *A New History of Southeast Asia* (New York: Palgrave-Macmillan, 2010), 19.

[83] Barbara A. West, *Encyclopedia of the Peoples of Asia and Oceania* (New York: Facts on File, 2009), 222.

[84] Meyer, 62-63.

85 Bình Giang, "This stele found at Tháp Mười in Đồng Tháp Province, Vietnam and now located in the Museum of History in Ho Chi Minh City is one of the few extant writings that can be attributed confidently to the kingdom of Funan. The text is in Sanskrit, written in Grantha alphabet of the Pallava dynasty, dated to the mid-5th century AD, and tells of a donation in honour of Vishnu by a Prince Gunavarman of the Kaundinya lineage," photograph, https://www.commons.wikimedia.org/wiki/File%3A Funan_stele.JPG, (accessed November 22, 2015).

Champa

To the east of Funan was Champa, situated in the southern and central regions of Vietnam. This kingdom also began as an Indian state. During the first century AD, Indian traders traveled to Champa by way of sea routes. Some of these merchants took up residency in Champa and by so doing introduced Indian culture to the early Cham people. A rock inscription, called by archaeologists a stele, records that a Hindu man named Sri Mara founded the Champa Kingdom in about the third century AD. As with Funan, both Buddhism and Hinduism were practiced in Champa with a preference to Hinduism. For example, in accordance with Hindu beliefs, many Chams practiced yoga and viewed cows as sacred creatures.[86]

By 192 AD, the Champa kingdom was well-established. At one point, the kingdom reached into northern Vietnam and even into southern China after they had successfully defeated the Chinese of the Han Dynasty who were ruling over these regions. China, though, was able to regain these territories. After the Vietnamese of northern Vietnam won their independence from China in 939 AD, the Champa Kingdom engaged, beginning in 979 AD, in a series of battles with the Vietnamese. Intermittent war between the Champa Kingdom and Vietnam lasted from 979 to 1470 when the Kingdom of Champa was defeated by the Vietnamese. The defeat caused many of the Cham people to flee their lands. Currently, only around 100,000 Vietnamese can trace their ancestry to the ancient Cham people.[87] The map on page 56 shows, c. 1100 AD, where Champa was in today's southern Vietnam, early Vietnam in the north, and the Khmer empire in the west.

---

[86] Meyer, 63; Ebrey, Walthall, and Palais, 28.
[87] West, 157-159.

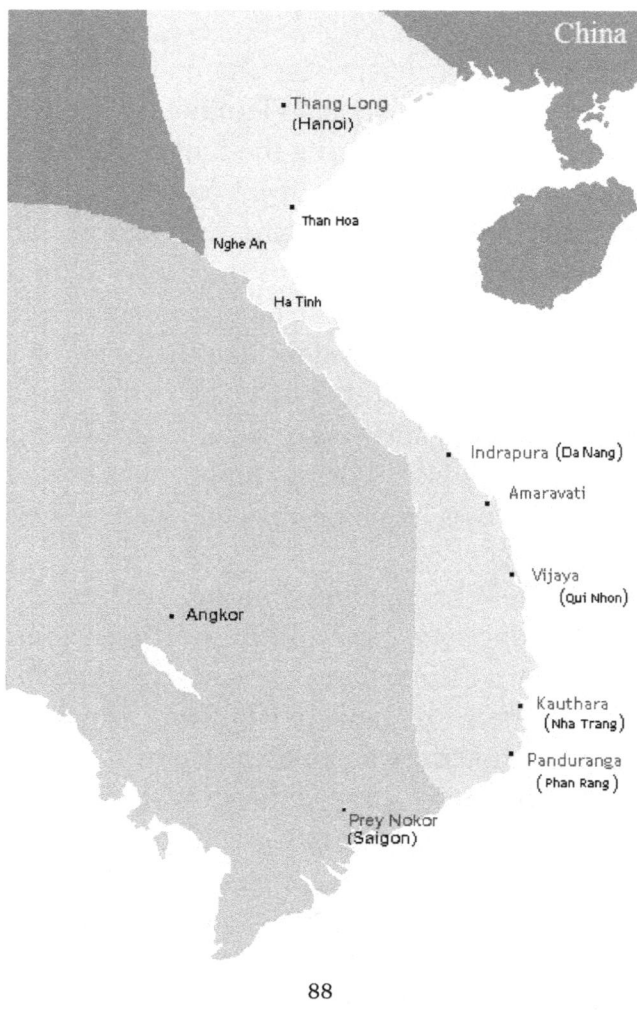

[88] Created by C. Glassey, based on maps found in DK Atlas of World History and the Times Atlas of World History, "Southeast Asia circa 1100 C.E. showing the approximate areas of control for the Dai-Viet (Vietnam), Champa, and Khmer Empires. Note: Control of the regions away from the coast of Vietnam was more nominal than real except along the Red River," photograph, https://commons.wikimedia.org/wiki/File%3AVietnamChampa1.gif, (accessed November 22, 2015).

Chenla

The Chenla people were once ruled by the Funan Empire. They became a kingdom when they defeated the Funan Empire around 550 AD. During these early periods, Hinduism was the dominant religion of the Chenla people. In the 600s, the Chenla kingdom promoted Mahayana Buddhism over Hinduism. During the 700s, the Chenla kingdom divided into two separate kingdoms. In this later period of the Chenla kingdom, Buddhism began to gain prominence. Around 790 AD, the Javanese defeated the Chenla kingdoms. In 802, a Khmer kingdom was established in what is now southern Cambodia. The Khmer were able to defeat the Javanese and place the former Chenla territories under their rule.[89]

Khmer Kingdom

King Jayavarman II was the first king of the Khmer kingdom of Angkor of modern-day Cambodia, establishing his kingdom in 802. Jayavarman II was a devout Hindu who believed he was a reincarnation of the Hindu God Shiva.[90] In 950 AD, the Khmer Kingdom expanded after it successfully invaded Champa and took over the Champa Kingdom. In so doing, the Khmers gained control of what is now central Vietnam. A shift from Hinduism to Buddhism was greatly encouraged when King Jayavarman VII (reigned 1181-1219) converted to Theravada Buddhism.[91]

---

[89] West, 160-161.
[90] Ebrey, Walthall, and Palais, 37.
[91] West, 390.

Vietnam

When the Qin Dynasty came to an end in 206 BC, northern Vietnam was formed into a kingdom called Nam Viet by the former Qin General Zhao Tuo, who is also known by the Vietnamese as Trieu Da.[92] An independent Vietnam ended when the Han Dynasty, led by Emperor Wu, conquered Vietnamese land in 111 BC. The Chinese ruled over regions of Vietnam until the early 900s when China's Tang Dynasty ended in 907. This thousand-year rule by the Chinese over the Vietnamese included short phases when Vietnamese leaders successfully resisted Chinese rule. One of the most famous were the Trung sisters of the first century AD.

The Trung Sisters were aristocratic Northern Vietnamese. The husband of Trung Trac, the oldest sister, was executed for protesting an increase of taxes by the Chinese. This caused Trung Trac and her sister to revolt against Chinese rule. They were joined by other aristocrats and by peasants. Their revolt took the Chinese occupiers by surprise and the Chinese withdrew. After the Chinese had retreated, Trung Trac was appointed Queen. She ruled with her sister, however, for only two years. Their reign ended when the Chinese sent troops into Vietnam. These troops restored Chinese rule over Vietnam, and the two sisters were either executed or committed suicide.[93] Other prominent resisters to Chinese rule include Lady Trieu Thi Trinh, Ly Bi, Trieu Viet Vuong, Mai Hac De, and Phung Hung. Similar to the Trung Sisters, Lady Trieu of the third century was also a young, strong-willed woman who refused to accept Chinese

---

[92] Ebrey, Walthall, and Palais, 53.
[93] Craig Lockhard, *Southeast Asia in World History* (Oxford: Oxford University Press, 2009), 29-30.

domination. According to an eighteenth-century account, writes David G. Marr:

> Trieu Thi Trinh was nine feet tall [... had] a voice like a temple bell, and was able to eat several pecks of rice and walk five hundred leagues in a single day. Yet she was also said to possess a beauty that could shake the soul of any man. [... She once said to her brother] "I only want to tide the wind and walk the waves, slay the big whale of the Eastern Sea, clean up our frontiers, and save the people from drowning. Why should I imitate others, bow my head, stoop over and be a slave? Why resign myself to menial housework?"[94]

During its prolonged contact with China, the Vietnamese were introduced by the Chinese to philosophies and beliefs that are central to China namely Daoism, Buddhism and Confucianism.[95] In 907, Vietnam finally regained its independence from China and developed as a separate political entity up until 1407 when China's Ming Dynasty conquered the Vietnamese and even set about to end a separate Vietnamese identity. Needless to say, they did not succeed.[96]

---

[94] David G. Marr, *Vietnamese Tradition on Trial, 1920-1945* (Berkeley: University of California Press, 1981), 198-199.

[95] M.C. Ricklefs, Bruce Lockhart, Albert Lau, Portia Reyes, and Maitrii Aung-Thwin *A New History of Southeast Asia* (New York: Palgrave-Macmillan, 2010), 32-33; Craig Lockhard, *Southeast Asia in World History* (Oxford: Oxford University Press, 2009), 28.

[96] Lockhard, 62.

~ Vietnamese Honoring the Trung Sisters ~

Quiz 4

1-4. Describe in at least four ways how, around the time of the Han Dynasty, China influenced South East Asian Cultures.

---

[97] Press and Information Office, Embassy of the Republic of Vietnam, "Procession of Elephants in the Hai Ba Trung Parade in Saigon, 7 March 1957," photograph, https://www.commons.wikimedia.org/wiki/File:HaiBaTrung.JPG, (accessed November 22, 2015).

5. How did Emperor Wu encourage a merit-based system for the selection of government officials?

6-8. Describe three influential factors which enabled Wang Mang to establish his short lived Xin Dynasty.

9-10. Compare and contrast Ban Zhao's teaching on women in *Lessons for Women* with St. Paul's teaching for women in Ephesians chapter five.

11. Describe the Sinification and Indianization of South Eastern Asian Cultures. (Sinification means the spread of Chinese culture. Similarly, Indianization means the spread of culture from India.) In your response include the following: traders, priests, Buddhism, Hinduism, Chinese philosophical thought, and a description of one of the following notable people: Kaundinya, Sri Mara, King Jayavarman II, Trung Sisters, and Lady Trieu.

Chapter 5: East Asia: Foreign Conquest and Influence

Introduction

During the 1200s, China, Korea, and South East Asia faced the terrifying foreign threat posed by the Mongols. Later, South East Asia came into contact with traders from another powerful foreign culture, the Islamic culture. For reasons of trade as well, western European countries also expressed pronounced interest in gaining influence over Eastern cultures. Christian missionaries followed in the wake of these western merchants.

Mongol Rule in China and Korea

The Mongols are an East-Central Asian ethnic people. The dark area in the map on page 64 indicates where modern-day Mongolia is located and where the Mongols comprised the majority of the population. The surrounding line denotes the boundaries of the vast Mongolian empire during the 1200's. As can be seen it once covered both China and Korea.

The Liao dynasty (907-1125) was an empire that ruled over Mongolia, an eastern Russian region, and northern China and Korea. During the time of its rule, central and southern China were ruled by a rapid succession of dynasties and kingdoms all of which came to an end around the time of China's Song Dynasty (960-1279).[99] The Liao dynasty ended in 1125 after the Manchurian Jurchen tribe successfully rebelled against Liao rule. A quasi-lawless state of uncer-

---

[98] Author not identified, "The orange line shows the extent of the Mongol Empire in the late 13th century. The red areas are the places dominated by [modern day] ethnic Mongol[s] in Mongolia, Russia, and China," map, https://www.commons.wikimedia.org/wiki/File:Mongols-map.png (accessed November 24, 2015).

[99] Patricia Ebrey, Anne Walthall, and James Palais, *East Asia: A Cultural, Social, and Political History* (Belmont: Wadsworth, 2009), 91, 129, and appendix.

tainty followed the collapse of the Liao dynasty.[100] During this time, around 1162, a baby boy named Temujin was born to a Mongolian woman. In 1206, Temujin united the nomadic Mongolian people into a vast empire. He eventually became known as Chinggis Khan or Genghis Khan (1162-1227), which means Fierce or Firm Ruler.

Mongol Invasions into South East Asia

During the 1200s, the Mongols attempted to conquer South East Asia as well but with little sustaining success. From 1281 to 1285, the Mongols aimed at overtaking the Vietnamese. They were defeated by a Vietnamese and Cham alliance, which succeeded in beating back the Mongols. The Vietnamese general Tran Hung Dao lead the anti-Mongol forces. Before leading these forces, the Vietnamese king Tran Nhan Tong asked the general if the Vietnamese should surrender to the Mongols in order to be saved from almost certain destruction. Tran Hung Dao is reputed to have replied, "But what will become of the lands of our ancestors, the temples of our elders? If You wish to surrender, order my head to be severed first."[101] This strong response motivated the king to defend his land with Tran Hung Dao in the lead. The soldiers under Tran Hung Dao's command tattooed on their arms "Death to the Mongols."[102]

A few years later, in 1287, the Mongols invaded the Kingdom of Pagan located in modern-day Myanmar (Burma). This invasion was short-lived since the Mongols were unaccustomed to the tropical weather of South East

---

[100] Timothy May, *The Mongol Conquests in World History* (London: Reaktion Books Ltd, 2012), 27-37.

[101] Henry Kamm, *Dragon Ascending: Vietnam and the Vietnamese* (New York: Arcade Publishing, 1996), 75.

[102] Kamm, 76.

Asia and withdrew north to China. The Mongol naval invasion of Java, an island of modern day Indonesia, was also unsuccessful.[103]

Tran Hung Dao Temple of Saigon

104

---

[103] Craig Lockhard, *Southeast Asia in World History* (Oxford: Oxford University Press, 2009), 48-49.

[104] Xiaoao, "Tran Hung Dao temple, 1st district, Saigon," photograph, https://www.commons.wikimedia.org/wiki/File%3A Tranhungdaostatem.jpg (accessed December 22, 2015).

Islam in the Malay World

Islam gained great influence over the Malay people who are descendants of the Mongolians. A few thousand years ago, the Malay people migrated from India and other regions of Asia to settle in South East Asia. The nations that constitute the majority of Malay people of South East Asia are Indonesia, Malaysia, and the Philippines. The Malays are also present in southern Thailand and Brunei. Currently, the Malay people make up around twenty percent of the Islamic world. Not all, though, are Islamic. This is most noticeable in the Philippines where 90 percent of the population are Christians, with the majority being Catholic.[105]

Before the advent of Islam, the South East Asian lands of the Malay people were highly influenced by two religions from India, Buddhism and Hinduism. These two religions competed with one another. The South East Asian islands were first introduced to religions from India when the people from India established settlements on the islands. At times the relationship between Buddhism and Hinduism was expressed by tension and other times the two religions blended with each other and with the natural religions of the native people. During the seventh century, a distinctly Buddhist Srivijaya Empire (650-1377) came to power. It was followed in the 1300s by the Hindu Majapahit empire (1293-1527).[106] Following are maps of these two empires in land mainly associated with modern-day Indonesia and Malaysia.

---

[105] Robert Day McAmis, *Malay Muslims: The History and Challenge of Resurgent Islam in Southeast Asia* (Grand Rapids: William B. Eerdmans Publishing Co., 2002), 3-4.

[106] McAmis, 7-8.

Fr. Peter Samuel Kucer, MSA

The Buddhist Srivijaya Empire (700s)

---

¹⁰⁷ Gunawan Kartapranata, "Location of Srivijaya, Own work by uploader, redrawn from Munoz "Early Kingdoms of the Indonesian Archipelago and the Malay Peninsula" page 128
Maximum extent of Srivijaya Empire around 8th century. Expanding from Sumatra, Central Java, to Malay Peninsula. The arrows show the series of Srivijayan expedition and conquest, in diplomatic alliances, military campaign, or naval raids," map, https://commons.wikimedia.org/wiki/File%3ASrivijaya_Empire.svg, (accessed December 22, 2015).

Majapahit Empire (1300s)

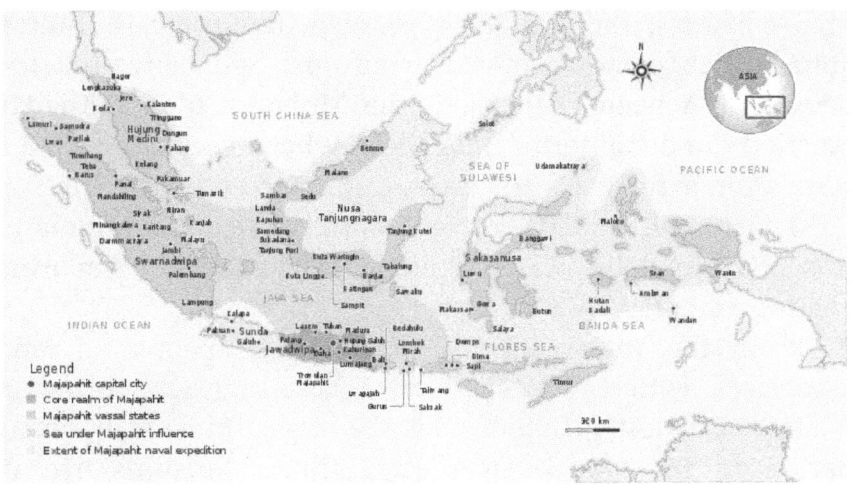

108

The Islamic influence in South East Asia was prepared by Arab traders who sailed to East Asia. According to Chinese records, the Arabs settled in Sumatra in 674 AD. (Sumatra is an island of western Indonesia.) After Muhammad (570-632 AD) united Arab tribes with his Islamic religion, Arab traders who were Islamic established settlements in East Asia and South East Asia. It is debated among scholars to what extent, if any, these Islamic traders sought out converts to Islam. It

---

108 Gunawan Kartapranata, "Location of Majapahit Empire, The Nusantara Archipelago during the height of Majapahit Empire in XIV century. The dot is Trowulan; Majapahit capital city. The darker area is the core realm of Majapahit on eastern part of Java. The light areas are vassal states of Majapahit mentioned in Nagarakretagama. The pale areas make up the outer realm or independent states from Majapahit. The very dark area on the coast was under influence or effective control of Majapahit. The light is the extent of Majapahit naval expedition." map, https://www.commons.wikimedia.org/wiki/File%3AMajapahit_Empire.svg, (accessed December 22, 2015). Go to the link for color-coding.

was not until the 1200s when the people of the island of Sumatra converted to Islam. According to a classic text of Malay history, the *Annals of Acheen*, in 1204 AD "Sultan Johan Shah came from the windward and converted the people of Acheen (Acheh) to the Mohammedan faith. He married the daughter of Baludri of Acheen and by her had a son...after a reign of 30 years ...was succeeded by his son Sultan Ahmad."[109] This conversion of the people of Sumatra was confirmed by Marco Polo in 1292 when he reported visiting Sumatra.

From the 1200s till the present day, people of land associated with Indonesia have increasingly converted to Islam.[110] Currently, Indonesia is the largest Muslim-majority nation in the world. Over 197 million Muslims live in Indonesia.[111] Two other South East Asian countries which also have a Muslim majority are Malaysia and Brunei. Large Muslim minorities are present throughout South East Asia including in Singapore, Thailand, and the Philippines. Among all the religions of South East Asia, Islam has the most number of adherents, about 250 million. Hussin Mutalib explains that "[o]f the estimated 1.3 billion Muslims in the world, about 60 percent live in Asia.[112] South East Asia, then, has about 1/3 of all Asian Muslims.

A country where Islam was prevented from expanding is

---

[109] Robert Day McAmis, *Malay Muslims: The History and Challenge of Resurgent Islam in Southeast Asia* (Grand Rapids: William B. Eerdmans Publishing Co., 2002), 12.

[110] McAmis, 9-16.

[111] This figure is based on the 2015 population estimate and the 2010 estimate of Muslims in Indonesia. "Indonesia," CIA The World Factbook, https://www.cia.gov/library/publications/the-world-factbook/geos/id.html, (accessed December 23, 2015).

[112] Hussin Mutalib, *Islam in Southeast Asia* (Singapore: Institute of Southeast Asian Studies, 2008), 1.

the Philippines, which is a predominantly Catholic country. When the Portuguese explorer Ferdinand Magellan, at the service of the Spanish King, arrived in 1521 to what is now known as the Philippines, he planted a wooden cross and asserted that all of the islands were the property of Spain.[113] The islands were, consequently, named after the Spanish King Philip II. Following the trading routes established by Magellan and others, Catholic missionaries evangelized the Filipinos. Due to the missionary presence backed by the Spanish King, the presence of Islam greatly decreased and was replaced by Catholicism. Today, the Philippines is about 81 percent Catholic. The largest minority religion in the Philippines is Islam coming in at 5 percent of the population.[114]

Western Trade, Christianity and East Asia

The discovery of new trade routes to Asia prompted a competition between Portugal and Spain over who could colonize the Asian lands. In an attempt to settle the dispute and to bring order to missionary activity, Pope Alexander VI issued three bulls. In his 1493 bull *Inter caetera* he defined Spain's territorial rights by stating:

> Alexander, bishop, servant of the servants of God, to the illustrious sovereigns, our very dear son in Christ, Ferdinand, king, and our very dear daughter in Christ, Isabella, queen of Castile, Leon, Aragon, Sicily, and Granada, health and apostolic benediction. Among other

---

[113] Mutalib, 65.
[114] Mutalib, 6; "Philippines," CIA Factbook, https://www.cia.gov/library/publications/the-world-factbook/geos/rp.html (accessed December 24, 2015).

works well pleasing to the Divine Majesty and cherished of our heart, this assuredly ranks highest, that in our times especially the Catholic faith and the Christian religion be exalted and be everywhere increased and spread, that the health of souls be cared for and that barbarous nations be overthrown and brought to the faith itself. ... In the islands and countries already discovered are found gold, spices, and very many other precious things of divers kinds and qualities. Wherefore, as becomes Catholic kings and princes, after earnest consideration of all matters, especially of the rise and spread of the Catholic faith, as was the fashion of your ancestors, kings of renowned memory, you have purposed with the favor of divine clemency to bring under your sway the said mainlands and islands with their residents and inhabitants and to bring them to the Catholic faith. ... And, in order that you may enter upon so great an undertaking with greater readiness and heartiness endowed with the benefit of our apostolic favor, we, of our own accord, not at your instance nor the request of anyone else in your regard, but of our own sole largess and certain knowledge and out of the fullness of our apostolic power, by the authority of Almighty God conferred upon us in blessed Peter and of the vicarship of Jesus Christ, which we hold on earth, do by tenor of these presents, should any of said islands have been found by your envoys and captains, give, grant, and assign to you and your heirs and successors, kings of Castile and Leon, forever, together with all their dominions, cities, camps, places, and villages, and all rights, jurisdictions, and appurtenances, all islands and mainlands found and to be found, discovered and to be discovered towards the west and south, by drawing and establishing a line from the Arctic pole, namely the north, to the Antarctic pole, namely the south, no matter whether the said mainlands and islands are found and to be found in the direction of India or towards any other quarter, the said line to be distant one hundred leagues towards the west and south from any of the islands commonly known as the Azores and Cape Verde. With this proviso however that none of the islands and mainlands, found and to be found, discovered and to be discovered, beyond that said line towards the west and south, be in the actual possession of any Christian king or prince up to the birthday of our Lord Jesus Christ just past from which the present year one thousand four hundred and ninety-three begins."[115]

Influenced by Pope Alexander VI's concern that missionary activity take place in an orderly manner, the following year in 1494 the Treaty of Tordesillas was signed between Spain and Portugal. This treaty established trading and colonizing rights for Portugal and Spain. Building upon the Treaty of Tordesillas, the Treaty of Saragossa (1529) further divided up the entire known world between these two European powers. According to the two treaties, Portugal was allowed to trade with and colonize the lands to the east of their established lines, and Spain was allowed to trade with and colonize the lands to the west of the lines. These treaties only made sense as long as Portugal and Spain were the only European countries seeking to establish oversea empires. As other European nations joined in the race to establish their dominance throughout the world, these treaties began to be ignored. Finally, in 1750, the Treaty of

---

[115] "The Bull *Inter Caetera* (Alexander VI), May 4, 1493," Native Web, http://www.nativeweb.org/pages/legal/indig-inter-caetera.html, (accessed December 24, 2015).

Madrid overturned the Treaty of Tordesillas.[116]

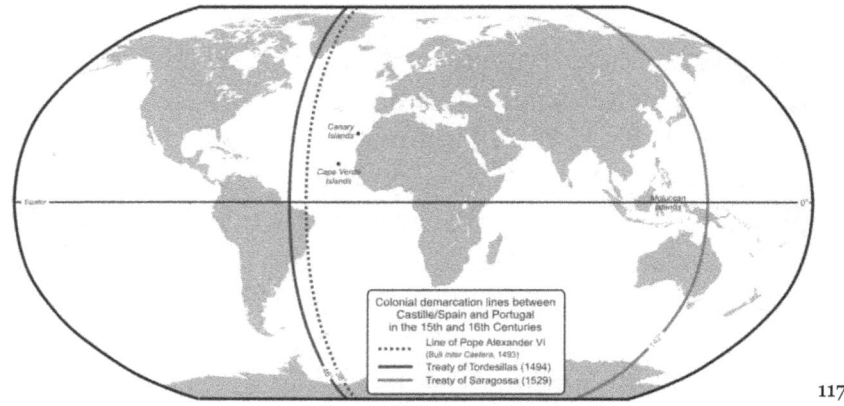

Below is an excerpt from the 1494 Treaty of Tordesillas. When reading it, compare and contrast it with Alexander's VI's 1493 papal bull *Inter caetera*:

> ... Thereupon it was declared by the above-mentioned representatives of the aforesaid King and Queen of Castile, Leon, Aragon, Sicily, Granada, etc., and of the aforesaid King of Portugal and the Algarves, etc.:
> [I.] That, whereas a certain controversy exists between the said lords, their constituents, as to what lands, of all those discovered in the ocean sea up to the present day, the date of this treaty, pertain to each one of the said

---

[116] Melvin E. Page, *Colonialism: An International Social, Cultural, and Political Encyclopedia*, Volume One: A-M (Santa Barbara: ABC CLIO, Inc., 2003), 585-586, 774.

[117] Lencer, "Lines dividing the non-Christian world between Spain and Portugal: the 1494 Tordesillas meridian (on the left) and the 1529 Zaragoza anti-meridian (on the right)," map, https://en.wikipedia.org/wiki/Treaty_of_Tordesillas#/media/File:Spain_and_Portugal.png (accessed December 24, 2015). See link for color.

parts respectively; therefore, for the sake of peace and concord, and for the preservation of the relationship and love of the said King of Portugal for the said King and Queen of Castile, Aragon, etc., it being the pleasure of their Highnesses, they, their said representatives, acting in their name and by virtue of their powers herein described, covenanted and agreed that a boundary or straight line be determined and drawn north and south, from pole to pole, on the said ocean sea, from the Arctic to the Antarctic pole. This boundary or line shall be drawn straight, as aforesaid, at a distance of three hundred and seventy leagues west of the Cape Verde Islands, being calculated by degrees, or by any other manner as may be considered the best and readiest, provided the distance shall be no greater than above said. And all lands, both islands and main lands, found and discovered already, or to be found and discovered hereafter, by the said King of Portugal and by his vessels on this side of the said line and bound determined as above, toward the east, in either north or south latitude, on the eastern side of the said bound provided the said bound is not crossed, shall belong to, and remain in the possession of, and pertain forever to, the said King of Portugal and his successors. And all other lands, both islands and main lands, found or to be found hereafter, discovered or to be discovered hereafter, which have been discovered or shall be discovered by the said King and Queen of Castile, Aragon, etc., and by their vessels, on the western side of the said bound, determined as above, after having passed the said bound toward the west, in either its north or south latitude, shall belong to, and remain in the possession of, and pertain forever to, the said King and Queen of Castile, Leon, etc., and to their successors.

[2.] Item, the said representatives promise and affirm by virtue of the powers aforesaid, that from this date no ships shall be dispatched ... for the purpose of discovering and seeking any main lands or islands, or for the purpose of trade, barter, or conquest of any kind. But should it come to pass that the said ships of the said King and Queen of Castile, Leon, Aragon, etc., on sailing thus on this side of the said bound, should discover any main lands or islands in the region pertaining, as above said, to the said King of Portugal, such main lands or islands shall pertain to and belong forever to the said King of Portugal and his heirs, and their Highnesses shall order them to be surrendered to him immediately. And if the said ships of the said King of Portugal discover any islands and mainlands in the regions of the said King and Queen of Castile, Leon, Aragon, etc., all such lands shall belong to and remain forever in the possession of the said King and Queen of Castile, Leon, Aragon, etc., and their heirs, and the said King of Portugal shall cause such lands to be surrendered immediately.[118]

Prior to the discovery of new trade routes by sailing east around Africa or by sailing West around South America, Asia was reached by the Silk Routes about which the Venetian merchant Marco Polo (1254-1324) wrote. The silk after which these trade routes were named was extracted from silk worms raised in China. The Chinese had mastered silk cultivation 2000 to 3000 years before the birth of Christ.[119]

---

[118] "Treat between Spain and Portugal concluded at Tordesillas; June 7, 1494," Yale Law School, Lillian Goldman Law Library, The Avalon Project, http://www.avalon.law.yale.edu/15th_century/mod001.asp (accessed December 24, 2015).

[119] Xinru Liu, *The Silk Road in World History* (Oxford: Oxford University Press, 2010), 1, 10, 20.

East and South East Asian History

In time, land and sea trade routes developed between China and the Mediterranean lands. During the first century AD, the Roman Pliny the Elder (23-79 AD) in his *Natural History* referred to the great quantities of East Asian silk that the Romans had recently obtained by way of the Silk Routes.[120]

Christian missionaries followed the Silk Routes in order to bring Christ to East Asia. According to the Mar Thomas church of India, St. Thomas the Apostle not only evangelized India in the 60s AD but also travelled to China and then returned to India.[121] This traditional claim received some

---

[120] Liu, 1, 10, 20.

[121] The Mar Thomas Church of Saint Thomas Christians trace the origins of their rite back to the apostle Thomas. Currently, some of the Christians are Orthodox, others are Catholics, and still other groups who do not identify themselves as Orthodox or as Catholic. The chart below displays these divisions.

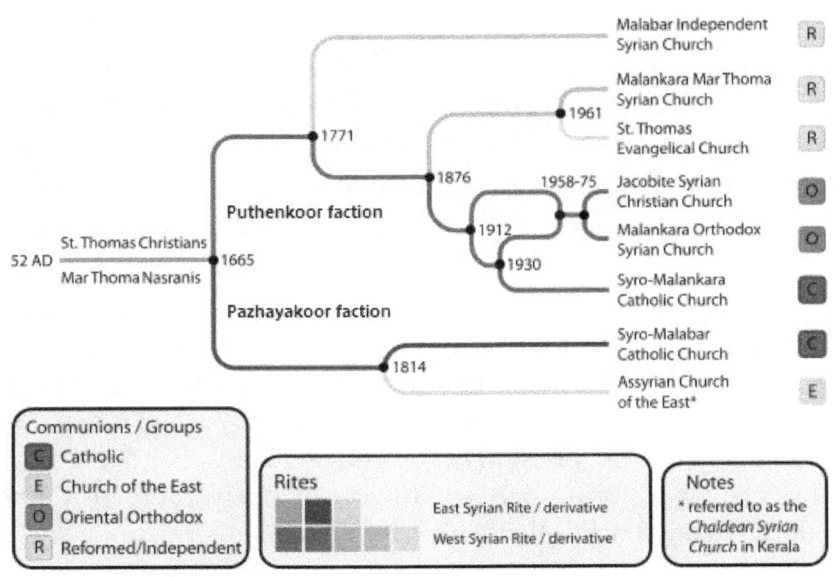

archaeological support when bas-relief sculptures on a rock face at Kongwangshan, near Lianyungang city of China's Jiangsu Province were reexamined by scholars. Some scholars now think that these sculptures are not Buddhist figures but rather are depictions of early Christians including the Apostle Thomas and the Blessed Mother. The sculptures have been dated to the time of the Chinese Mingdi emperor (r. 57-75 AD) who lived at the time of the Apostle Thomas.[122]

It wouldn't be until a number of centuries later when Eastern Christians, from a heretical group called the Nestorians, began evangelizing China in an orderly manner. Their activity was affirmed in the 1620s AD when a nine-foot high marble stele was uncovered. The Chinese characters and Syriac letters on the stele describe the history of early Christianity in China. The author Jingling is identified as a Christian monk. The date he gives to the beginning of Chinese Christianity is 635 AD. The top of the stele is decorated with a lotus blossom out of which a cross is emerging. Below the flower is the title, "A Monument Commemorating the Propagation of Da-Qin (Syrian) Luminous Religion in China."[123] This also may be translated as "The Story of the Coming of the Religion of Light from the West to China."[124] Scholars are not in agreement on why this early form of Chinese Christianity did not last. By the end of the Tang dynasty in 907 Christianity had virtually dis-

---

St_Thomas_Christians_divisions.png: Joehoya3, "A chart describing the divisions within the St. Thomas Christians of Kerala," chart, https://commons.wikimedia.org/wiki/File%3ASt_Thomas_Christians_divisions.svg (accessed December 27, 2015).

[122] Daniel H. Bays, *A New History of Christianity in China* (Oxford: Wiley-Blackwell, 2012), 5.

[123] Bays, 7.

[124] Bays, 7.

appeared from China.[125] Many centuries later in the 1500s Jesuit Missionaries re-introduced Christianity to China.

~ Nestorian Chinese Stele ~

[125] Bays, 7-11.
[126] Nestorian monk Jingjing. Rubbing/drawing made by Henri Havret, or a local collaborator of his, "The Nestorian Stele entitled 大秦景教流行中國碑 "Stele to the propagation in China of the luminous religion of Daqin", was erected in China in 781," Rubbing/drawing, https://www.commons.wikimedia.org/wiki/

Quiz 5

1. (Five Points) Compare and contrast the Mongol invasion of East Asia with the Mongol invasion of South East Asia. Include the following in your response: Genghis Khan, the extent of the Mongolian empire during the 1200s, Tran Hung Dao, and the Mongol invasion of Pagan and Java.

2. (Seven Points) Briefly describe how the Malay people were influenced by Buddhism, Hinduism, Islam, and Christianity. Include the following in your answer: Arab traders, Islamic-Arab traders, Srivijaya Empire, Majapahit empire, Island of Sumatra, Indonesia, and the Philippines.

3. (Five Points) Identify the 1493 bull Inter Caetera and the Treaty of Tordesillas. Then, compare and contrast these two documents in at least three ways.

4. (Six Points) Trace the early Christian presence in China. Include the following in your response: silk cultivation, Silk Routes, Pliny the Elder, St. Thomas the Apostle, Nestorians, and the Nestorian Chinese Stele.

File%3ANestorian-Stele-Budge-plate-X.jpg, (accessed December 27, 2016).

Chapter 6: Trade and Evangelization (1400s-1700s)

Introduction

Extensive trading between East Asia and European countries took place during the so-called Age of Discovery of the late 15th century. This age was in part sparked by the Fall of Constantinople in 1453 to the Ottoman, Islamic Empire. Prior to its fall, Constantinople was the capital of the Eastern Roman Empire and served as a doorway through which traders entered in order to access the Silk Routes to Asia.

Upon gaining control over this key port city, the Ottoman Muslims began charging Europeans prohibitively high prices to cross over Ottoman controlled lands. This incentivized Europeans to seek out cheaper trade routes to Asia. The maps below demonstrate the importance of the city of Constantinople and land around it in relationship to the Silk Routes.

Fr. Peter Samuel Kucer, MSA

~ Constantinople and the Silk Routes ~

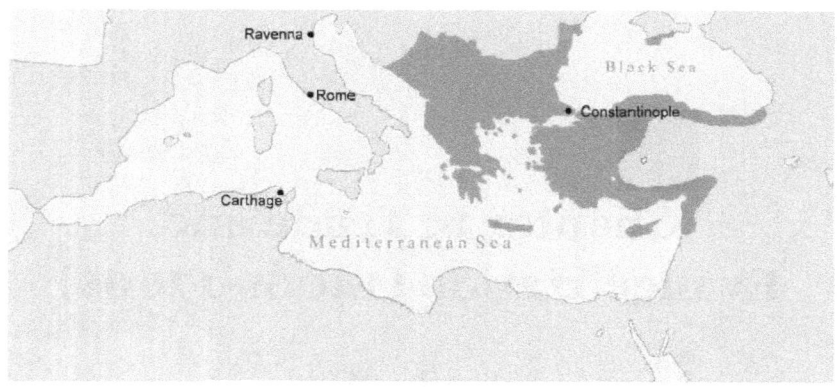

127

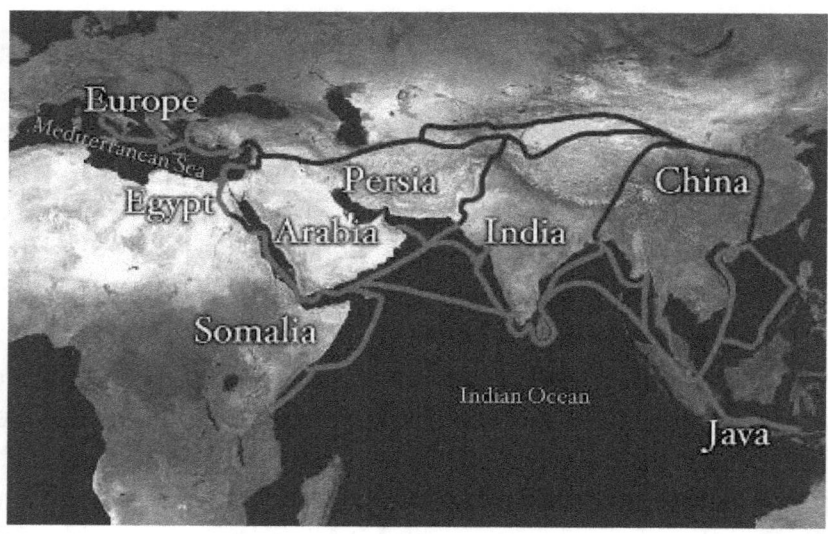

128

---

¹²⁷ Bigdaddy1204 (talk) (Uploads), "The Byzantine Empire under Manuel I, c. 1180," map, https://en.wikipedia.org/wiki/File:Byzantium@1180.jpg (accessed December 28, 2015).

¹²⁸ By Whole_world_-_land_and_oceans_12000.jpg: NASA/Goddard Space Flight Center derivative work:Splette derivative work:Bongan NASA - Visible Earth, images combined and scaled down by HighInBC (20 megabyte upload limit) NASA Visible Earth [Public domain], via Wikimedia Commons, http://www.

Some of the most important European discoverers of alternate trade routes to the East include Henry the Navigator, King John II of Portugal, Bartolomeu Dias, Vasco de Gama, Christopher Columbus, Ferdinand Magellan, and John Cabot. They all had the same goal of finding a new trade route to Asia. As will be evident, the Portuguese, who depended more on trade than other European countries, were the first to discover new trading routes and establish colonies in the process. The Spanish, the British, and the Dutch followed soon after.

Beginning with the Jesuits, Catholic missionaries traveled the new trading routes to Asia. The two most prominent of the early Jesuit missionaries to Asia were St. Francis Xavier and Matteo Ricci. Debate over what constituted acceptable means for evangelizing the Asian people divided missionaries. In the debate, Jesuits were more open than Dominicans and Franciscans to accepting certain features of Asian world views.

Asian countries also differed among one another over how to relate to European merchants, colonizers, and missionaries. China, Japan, and Korea all attempted to control the influence of foreigners on their lands by restricting trade to specific regions and by controlling or prohibiting missionary activity.

European Explorers in Search for the Orient

Inspired by reading Marco Polo's travels to Asia, the Portuguese Prince Henry the Navigator (1394-1460) financed Atlantic Ocean expeditions around Africa with the hope of reaching Asia. Below are navigation routes he

---

commons.wikimedia.org/wiki/File%3ASilk_route_copy.jpg (accessed November 3, 2014). See link for color.

sponsored.

~ Navigation Routes sponsored by Henry the Navigator ~

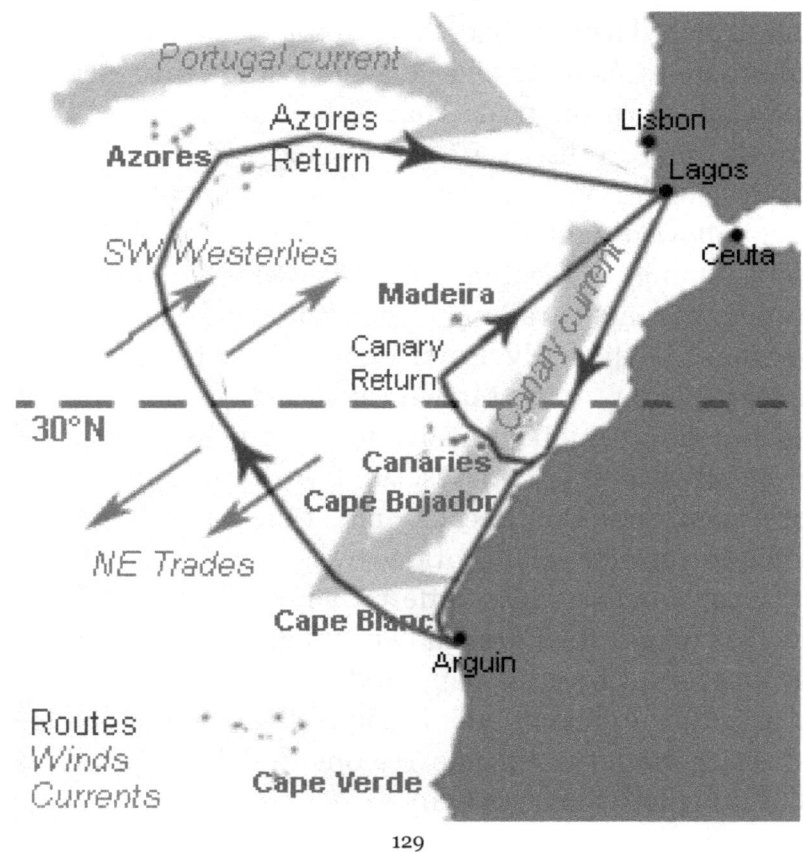

[129] Walrasiad, "General depiction of the winds (short arrows) and currents (shadow arrows) and the approximate sailing routes (long continuous arrows) of Portuguese navigators during the era of Henry the Navigator (c.1430-1460). The further south the ships go, the wider the return, and the more open sea sailing required. Based on the description in Gago Coutinho, 1951, *A Náutica dos Descobrimentos*," map, https://commons.wikimedia.org/wiki/File%3AHenrican_navigation_routes.gif, (accessed December 29, 2015). See link for color.

Shortly after Prince Henry's death, the King of Portugal, John II (1455-1495) also sponsored explorers with the same hope of discovering alternative trading routes to Asia. Bartolomeu Dias (1451-1500) was a particularly famous explorer who was backed by King John II. In 1488, Dias successfully sailed around the southern tip of Africa and landed at South Africa's Mossel Bay. Dias's exploration was tragically cut short when he and his ship were lost at sea in 1500.[130] Below is the route Dias successfully completed.

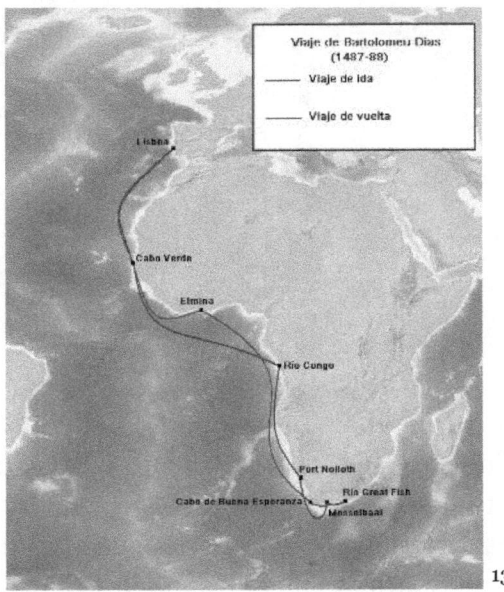

[131]

---

[130] A.R. Disney, *A History of Portugal and the Portuguese Empire: Volume Two, The Portuguese Empire* (Cambridge: Cambridge University Press, 2009), 38; James M. Anderson, *The History or Portugal* (Westport: Greenwood Press, 2000), 66.

[131] [GFDL (http://www.gnu.org/copyleft/fdl.html), CC-BY-SA-3.0 (http://creativecommons.org/licenses/by-sa/3.0/) or CC-BY-2.5 (http://creativecommons.org/licenses/by/2.5)], via Wikimedia Commons, http://www.commons.wikimedia.org/wiki/File

Dias's dream to reach Asia was fulfilled by another Portuguese explorer, Vasco de Gama (c. 1460-1524). In 1498, Vasco de Gama became the first European to navigate by sea to India. The route he discovered connected Europe and Asia with a non-land based route (recall the South East Asian adage that the land divides and the sea connects). The map below depicts the sea trade route he established.

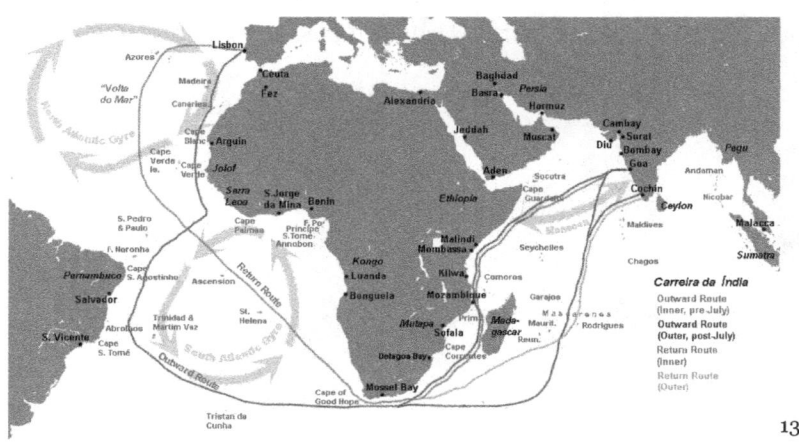

132

Unlike the previously mentioned Portuguese explorers, Christopher Columbus, John Cabot, and Ferdinand Magellan all attempted to discover a trade route to Asia by sailing west rather than east. Only Magellan was successful. Under the patronage of the Spanish Queen Isabella I and Ferdinand II, Columbus (c. 1450-1506) sailed westward in order to reach Asia but encountered a huge land mass, later called the Americas, that prevented him from going further.

%3ABartolomeu_Dias_Voyage.PNG (accessed November 3, 2014).

[132] Walrasiad (Own work) [CC-BY-3.0 (http://www.creativecommons.org/licenses/by/3.0)] via Wikimedia Commons, http://commons.wikimedia.org/wiki/File%3AMap_of_Portuguese_Carreira_da_India.gif (accessed November 4, 2014).

~ Voyages of Christopher Columbus ~

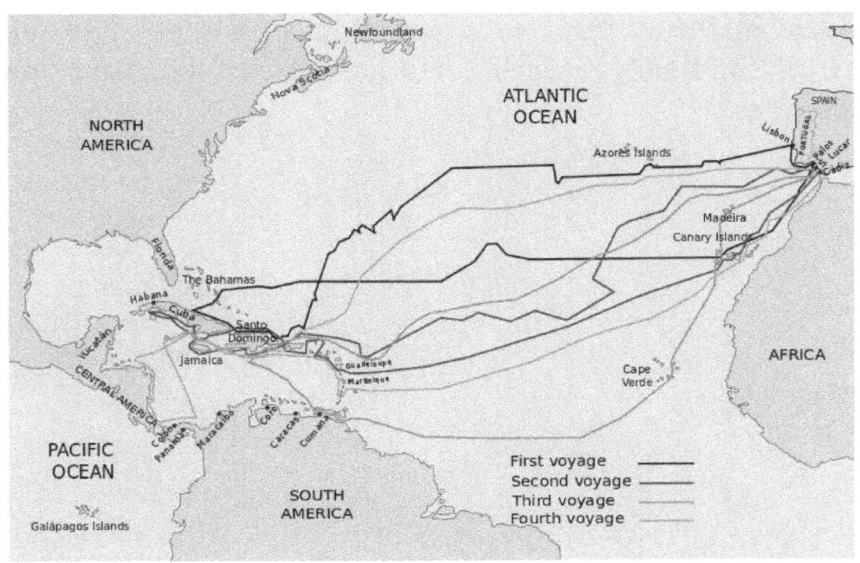

The Italian explorer John Cabot, also known as Zuan Chabotto, (c. 1450-c. 1499) attempted to find a Northwest Passage through America to Asia. In so doing, he became the first European since the Vikings to set foot on mainland North America. Other notable explorers who shared the goal of Cabot include Henry Hudson, Jacques Cartier, Rene-Robert Cavelier and Sieur de La Salle. Due to the massive size of America, none of them succeeded. Sponsored by King Charles I of Spain, the Portuguese explorer Ferdinand

---

[133] By Viajes_de_colon.svg: Phirosiberia derivative work: Phirosiberia (Viajes_de_colon.svg) [CC-BY-SA-3.0-2.5-2.0-1.0 (http://creativecommons.org/licenses/by-sa/3.0), CC-BY-SA-3.0-2.5-2.0-1.0 (http://creativecommons.org/licenses/by-sa/3.0) or GFDL (http://www.gnu.org/copyleft/fdl.html)], via Wikimedia Commons, http://commons.wikimedia.org/wiki/File%3AViajes_de_colon_en.svg (accessed November 4, 2014).

Magellan (c. 1480-1521) attempted to reach Asia by sailing south west around South America. En route, he died in a battle in the Philippines. Continuing on without him, his expedition finally reached South East Asia as the map below indicates.[134]

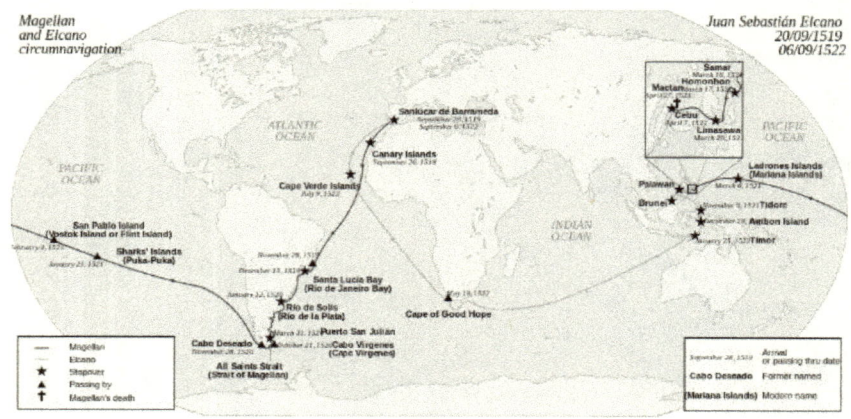

Trade and Colonization

The Portuguese and the Spanish were the first to establish trading posts, and in the case of Spain a colony, in East Asia. When the world balance of power shifted in favor of England and her allies, the English and the Dutch people

---

[134] Nancy Smiler Levinson, *Magellan: And the First Voyage around the World* (New York: Houghton Mifflin Co., 2001), 33-36, 87-96.

[135] y Magellan_Elcano_Circumnavigation-fr.svg: Sémhur derivative work: Uxbona (Magellan_Elcano_Circumnavigation-fr.svg) [CC-BY-SA-3.0-2.5-2.0-1.0 (http://creativecommons.org/licenses/by-sa/3.0) or GFDL (http://www.gnu.org/copyleft/fdl.html)], via Wikimedia Commons, http://commons.wikimedia.org/wiki/File%3AMagellan_Elcano_Circumnavigation-en.svg, (accessed November, 5, 2014).

of the Netherlands began establishing colonies in Asia. The defeat of the Spanish Armada in 1588 is representative of this change in world power.[136] In the previous chapter, the Spanish conquest of the Philippines was touched upon. This was the only region in East Asia that the Spanish were able to include in their empire. In contrast with Spain, Portugal was able to colonize many regions of Asia including locations in Malaysia and China.

After the Portuguese defeated the Chinese in Malacca, Malaysia, in 1511, Portuguese merchants traveled to China and established trade with the Chinese. Due to the reputation of the Portuguese for being impolite and not respectful of Chinese customs, the Ming Dynasty in 1521 restricted the Portuguese from entering China. The Portuguese king responded in 1523 by trying to establish a treaty. In the process, the Portuguese commissioned by their king engaged in a military skirmish with the Chinese. In 1557, Chinese officials avoided further confrontation with the Portuguese by allowing them to found a trading post on land near the Pearl River and close to the South China Sea. The Portuguese named the land Macao. Macao was overseen by the Portuguese until 1999 when sovereignty of Macau was officially transferred from Portugal to China.[137]

In the 1600s, the Dutch defeated the Portuguese presence in South East Asia. In so doing, the Dutch became the dominant European power in South East Asia. As a consequence, regions of Malaysia and Indonesia fell under Dutch rule.[138] In establishing their Asian colonies the Dutch,

---

[136] Craig Lockard, *Southeast Asia in World History*, (Oxford: Oxford University Press, 2009), 84.

[137] Patricia Ebrey, Anne Walthall, and James Palais, *East Asia: A Cultural, Social, and Political History* (Belmont: Wadsworth, 2009), 257.

[138] Lockard, 85.

unlike the Portuguese and Spanish, did not prioritize evangelizing the people with Christianity. One Dutch company particularly known for its great wealth and its monopolization of South East Asian trade was the Dutch East India Company. The company was known for ruthlessly killing native people in order to quell unrest.[139]

During the 1600s as well, the French successfully established themselves in Vietnam. French Catholic missionaries westernized Vietnam by inventing and introducing a Vietnamese alphabet based on the Roman alphabet. The Vietnamese had been relying upon the Chinese character system of writing.[140] In the 1800s, which will be presented in the next chapter, the British displaced the Dutch as the dominant power in Asia.

Catholic Missionaries

Many Catholic missionaries spoke out against and resisted the European brutal treatment of the Asian people. The Spanish Jesuit Catholic missionary St. Francis Xavier (1506-1552) criticized the Portuguese presence at Indonesia's Maluku Islands by asserting they had "an amazing capacity for inventing new tenses and participles" for the verb to steal.[141] After evangelizing people in India, in 1545 Francis Xavier landed in the Malaysian city of Malacca. He stayed in this region of South East Asia for eighteen months while preaching the Good News of Jesus Christ to the people of Malaysia and of Indonesia. At the end of eighteen months, he returned to India. While there he was inspired to travel to Japan.

---

[139] Lockard, 87.
[140] Lockard, 90.
[141] Lockard, 78.

In 1549, Francis Xavier sailed to Japan. He learned that in order to effectively evangelize the Japanese he needed to shed his poorly dressed appearance, which when he was in India appealed to the Indian sense of a holy poor man. The Japanese did not share this Indian connection of poverty with holiness. When in Japan, Francis Xavier, therefore, presented himself well-dressed before the Japanese ruler of Kyoto. He also introduced himself as a representative of the king of Portugal. Impressed by Francis Xavier, the ruler offered him protection and housing in a Buddhist monastery. With the backing of the Kyoto ruler, Francis Xavier baptized around two thousand Japanese. Once a core group was formed upon whom he could rely, Francis Xavier returned to India and stayed there for about four months before setting sail once again eastward. His final goal was to evangelize China. He did not obtain this goal, but instead became ill and died in Shang-chwan, an island near to the coast of China.[142]

The Italian Jesuit Matteo Ricci (1552-1610), who was one of the first Jesuits to evangelize China, was born in the same year that Francis Xavier died. Like Francis Xavier, Ricci spent a number of years in India before setting sail to the Portuguese-administered Chinese territory of Macao. There he began mastering the Chinese language and learning about the Chinese culture. When news of Ricci's knowledge of astronomy and skill in mapmaking reached the Chinese Emperor, Ricci was invited to see the emperor in China's Forbidden City.[143]

One way Ricci attempted to draw the Chinese to the Catholic faith was by adopting non-European ways and

---

[142] Kathleen Jones, *Butler's Lives of the Saints*, New Full Edition, December (Collegeville: The Liturgical Press, 1999), 26-30.

[143] Michela Fontana, *Matteo Ricci: A Jesuit in the Ming Court* (Lanham: Rowman & Littlefield Publishers, 2011), 200-212.

intellectual ideas that he thought were compatible with the Catholic faith. Other Jesuits also shared in this manner of evangelization. As mentioned previously, they met resistance from Dominican and Franciscan missionaries who complained to Rome. Issues of concern included the use of Confucian concepts when teaching Christianity and the acceptance by some Jesuits of the Chinese tradition of honoring the dead. In 1645, Pope Innocent X responded to these concerns by decreeing that the Chinese rites promoted by the Jesuits were forbidden.[144] In 1721, the Chinese emperor responded to Rome's assertion that the Chinese practice of ancestor veneration rites are not compatible with the Catholic faith by forbidding Christian missions in China.[145]

Currently, Rome is revisiting Ricci's missionary work in China, work that was appreciated by the Chinese more than by some influential European Catholics of Ricci's time. In 1984, Ricci was declared a "Servant of God." In 2010, the Cause of Beatification of Ricci was formally opened. An Historical Commission has been gathering together documents of Ricci in order to critically analyze them.[146] In 2013, the first stage for the beatification of Ricci was completed.[147]

---

[144] Fontana, 291-294.

[145] "Beatification Process Begins for Chinese Missionary Jesuit Father Matteo Ricci," Jesuits News Detail, http://jesuits.org/news-detail?TN=NEWS-20140219034957 (accessed January 1, 2016).

[146] "Father Matteo Ricci's Beatification Cause Reopened", Agenzia Fides, http://www.fides.org/en/news/25874?idnews=25874&lan=eng#.VF5r_-ktC1s (accessed November 8, 2014).

[147] Benoit Vermander, "Matteo Ricci and Xu Guangqi, two saints the Chinese Church deserves to venerate together," AsiaNews.it, http://www.asianews.it/news-en/Matteo-Ricci-and-

Both Pope Benedict XVI and Pope Francis have positively appraised Ricci's methods of evangelization. According to Benedict XVI, speaking on the fourth centenary of Ricci's death:

> Fr Ricci is a unique case of a felicitous synthesis between the proclamation of the Gospel and the dialogue with the culture of the people to whom he brought it; he is an example of balance between doctrinal clarity and prudent pastoral action. Not only his profound knowledge of the language but also his assumption of the lifestyle and customs of the cultured Chinese classes, the result of study and its patient, far-sighted implementation, ensured that Fr Ricci was accepted by the Chinese with respect and esteem, no longer as a foreigner but as the 'Master of the Great West'.[148]

In continuity with this appreciation of Ricci, Pope Francis stated in November, 2013, "We must always ask forgiveness and look with shame upon apostolic failures brought about by a lack of courage. I am thinking, for example, of the pioneering intuitions of Matteo Ricci which, at the time, were abandoned."[149] Carefully read the except below from Ricci's *The True Meaning of the Lord of Heaven*. This is an example of Ricci attempting to teach Catholic doctrine with Confucian

---

Xu-Guangqi,-two-saints-the-Chinese-Church-deserves-to-venerate-together-30667.html, (accessed January 1, 2016).

[148] Benedict XVI, "Papal Address on 400th Anniversary of Matteo Ricci's Death," Zenit, http://www.zenit.org/en/articles/papal-address-on-400th-anniversary-of-matteo-ricci-s-death (accessed January 1, 2016).

[149] Paul A. Zalonski, "Matteo Ricci Sainthood Cause Moves Ahead," Communion Blog, http://communio.stblogs.org/index.php/tag/matteo-ricci/ (accessed January 1, 2016).

concepts. What do you think of his attempt?

~ Mistaken Views about the Lord of Heaven ~

1. The Western scholar says: The work of creation is an enormous undertaking and it must have its own pivot; but this is established by the Lord of Heaven. If there were no first cause to serve as the source of phenomena, neither principle nor the Supreme Ultimate would be able to fill this role. I am sure that there initially must have been very profound reasons for the teachings concerning the Supreme Ultimate. I have read them, and I would not dare to cast aside these arguments in any casual manner. Perhaps I shall later be able to write another book in which I can discuss their important ideas.

101. The Chinese scholar says: From ancient times to the present the sovereigns and ministers of my country have known only that they should pay reverence to Heaven and Earth as if they were reverencing their fathers and mothers. They have therefore employed the ceremonial of state worship to sacrifice to them. If the Supreme Ultimate were the source of heaven and earth it would be the first ancestor of the world; and the first sages, emperors, and ministers of ancient times ought to have given priority to the worship of it. But, in fact, this was not the case. It is obvious, then, that the explanation given of the Supreme Ultimate is incorrect. You have argued the matter exhaustively, Sir, and your views are the same as those of the sages and worthies of ancient times.

102. The Western scholar says: Despite what you say, the teaching that Heaven and Earth are the two things most

honored is by no means easy to explain, since that which is most deserving of honor is unique and unparalleled. If we speak of "heaven" and "earth" we are talking about two things.

103. He who is called the Lord of Heaven in my humble country is He who is called Shang-ti (Sovereign on High) in Chinese. He is not, however, the same as the carved image of the Taoist Jade Emperor who is described as the Supreme Lord of the Black Pavilions of Heaven, for he was no more than a recluse on Wu-tang mountain. Since he was a man, how could he have been the Sovereign of heaven and earth?

104. Our Lord of Heaven is the Sovereign on High mentioned in the ancient [Chinese] canonical writings [as the following texts show]: Quoting Confucius, the Doctrine of the Mean says: "The ceremonies of sacrifices to Heaven and Earth are meant for the service of the Sovereign on High." Chu Hsi comments that the failure to mention Sovereign Earth [after Sovereign on High] was for the sake of brevity. In my humble opinion what Chung-ni [i.e. Confucius] intended to say was that what is single cannot be described dualistically. How could he have been seeking merely for brevity of expression?[150]

A few other heroic people who brought the Catholic faith to East Asia include Fr. Alessandro Valignano, Fr. Alexandre de Rhodes, and Yi Seung-hun. Building upon the missionary work of St. Francis Xavier, the Italian Jesuit Fr. Alessandro

---

[150] Matteo Ricci, "The True Meaning of the Lord of Heaven," Christendom Awake, http://www.christendom-awake.org/pages/dlancash/chineseworks/tmlh.html (accessed November 8, 2014).

Valignano (1539-1606) evangelized people of India, Japan, and China. During the latter part the sixteenth century, Valignano was the leading Jesuit missionary of Asia. As the Jesuit's canonical visitor of the Asian missions, Valignano helped to give direction to missions in India, China and Japan. He did this in a diplomatic manner. This style of his is evident in his establishment of the first Japanese embassy to Europe.[151] On June 4th, 1587, at the Goa Jesuit College the ambassador Hara Martinho praised Valignano in the following manner:

> Blessed are the eyes that see such things, and blessed are we who have seen them. But more blessed are you, Alexander great in virtue, for you were the principle cause of our participation in so much good. ... O Alexander greater far than Alexander the Great, you have conquered and pacified almost all India with the arms of Christ. There remains now only the world of Japan, no easy conquest to any other than Alexander.... Storm that country with the arms of God, conquer it with good works, wrest our fatherland from the enemy most cruel, and bring it to true freedom. [...] The Japanese call out to you, they long for you; the winds are favorable, the seas calm, the doors are open wide.[152]

In 1614, the missionary work that Valignano had overseen in Japan was greatly diminished when Jesuits were ordered to leave Japan. They were accused of disrupting Japan's Confucian social order. Some Jesuits responded by

---

[151] J.F. Moran, *The Japanese and the Jesuits: Alessandro Valignano in Sixteenth Century Japan* (London: Routledge, 1993), 1-6.

[152] Moran, 6.

going to Vietnam in order to evangelize there. The leading Jesuit missionary to Vietnam from this time was the French Jesuit, Fr. Alexandre de Rhodes (1591-1660). From 1627-1630, Alexandre brought over 6,700 Vietnamese into the Catholic Faith. A number of means he used to evangelize included writing a catechism for the Vietnamese and writing a Vietnamese dictionary complete with a Romanized alphabet. This is the alphabet the Vietnamese currently use.[153]

We will end with Yi Seung-hun, a missionary in Asia who was neither a Jesuit nor European. Yi Seung-hun (1756-1801) was the first Korean convert to Catholicism. He received baptism in 1784 from a French priest and former Jesuit living in Beijing, China. The reason why Yi Seung-hun was in Beijing was because for a number of years he and other Korean scholars had been studying Chinese writings on the Jesuits in Beijing. Their study motivated them to go to Beijing in 1784 in order to talk with the Jesuit priests. While there, Yi Seung-hun asked to be baptized. After being taught basic catechism, Yi Seung-hun was baptized by Fr. Jean-Joseph de Grammont with the Christian name of Peter (*Pierre*).

Before returning to his homeland of Korea, Yi Seung-hun obtained crosses and other items to give to his friends. Back in Korea, he, along with Yi Piek, formed a small Catholic community. In his zeal, he baptized a number of Koreans into the Catholic faith. In 1786, he even attempted to celebrate the Eucharist, which, since he was not ordained to the priesthood, was invalid, but he did not know this. By 1789, the Korean Catholic community had grown to about a thousand members. All of this occurred without priests, and

---

[153] Hugh Dyson Walker, *East Asia: A New History* (Bloomington: AuthorHouse, 2012), 313.

even without the benefit of a Bible. When governmental officials heard about Yi Seung-hun's Christian community, they attempted to eliminate what they perceived was a threat to their national security and unity. Between 1784 and 1794, over four hundred Korean Christians were publicly martyred. News of the plight of the Korean Christians reached the bishop of Beijing, Msgr. De Gouvea. He responded by sending a Chinese priest, Fr. James Chou Wen-Mo, to properly catechize the Korean Christians. In 1801, Fr. James Chou Wen-Mo was also martyred, but only after he had for five years properly instructed Korean Christians in the Catholic faith. At the time of his martyrdom, the Korean Catholic Church had grown to ten thousand members.[154]

---

[154] Samuel Hugh Moffett, *A History of Christianity in Asia*, Volume II (Maryknoll, New York: Orbis Books, 2005), 311-314.

Quiz 6

1. (Five Points) Explain why the fall of Constantinople motivated Europeans to find new trading routes to Asia. Include the following in your response: the date of the fall, Ottoman Empire, Silk Routes, western sea routes, eastern sea routes.

2. (Nine Points) Compare and contrast Bartolomeu Dias, and Vasco de Gama with Christopher Columbus, Ferdinand Magellan, and John Cabot. Include in your response the following: western sea routes, eastern sea routes, Northwest passage, the goal of all the explorers, and specific discoveries of each explorer.

3. (Eight Points) Contrast the current appraisal of the Servant of God Matteo Ricci missionary work in Asia with the appraisal of his work in the 1600s. Include in your response the following: Dominicans and Franciscans, two specific issues that were thought to be problematic, Innocent X, Chinese rites, Pope Benedict XVI, and Pope Francis.

4. (Six Points) Contrast how Korea was introduced to the Catholic faith with how China was introduced to the Catholic faith. Include the following in your response: Yi Seung-hun, Chinese Jesuits, the first baptisms in Korea, the attempted mass in Korea, priests and the bible.

Chapter 7: Western Imperialism (1800s-1900s)

Introduction

As described in the previous chapter, during the 1700s Europeans founded trading posts throughout Asia. The Spanish of the time were able to establish the first European colony in the Philippines. In the 1800s, European countries followed Spain's example by transforming many of their Asian trading posts into colonies. In the midst of this colonization, Britain emerged as the dominant European power. France, Russia, and the United States also imposed their will over Asia. At times, these great world powers competed with one another for dominance as was evident in the Crimean War (1853-1856), which Russia lost to an alliance that included the Ottoman Empire, Britain, France, and Piedmont-Sardinia. Even though the Crimean War had at least symbolically begun to determine who would control the Holy Land, Britain entered the war in order to diminish Russian expansion into East Asia.[155]

---

[155] Patricia Ebrey, Anne Walthall, and James Palais, *East Asia: A Cultural, Social, and Political History* (Belmont: Wadsworth, 2009), 296-303; Orlando Figes, *The Crimean War: A History* (New York: Henry Holt and Company, 2010), xviii-xxiii.

Fr. Peter Samuel Kucer, MSA

The British in Asia

From 1803 to 1815 in the Napoleonic Wars, Britain and France struggled with one another over who would be the foremost world power. During this conflict neither country invaded the other. Rather, each tried to reduce the influence the other country had in world politics. The British did this by taking control over regions that were either directly under French control and or ruled by French dominated countries specifically the Netherlands and Spain. This included locations in South East Asia. When Napoleon Bonaparte was finally defeated in the battle of Waterloo (1815), the British solidified their power throughout the world. In so doing, the British replaced the role of the Dutch who had been the number one European power in South East Asia.[156] In 1798, the Dutch-controlled Ceylon (currently Sri Lanka) became a British dominion. Similarly, between 1811 and 1816 the British took over the French-controlled Java (an island of Indonesia). In 1816, the British returned Java to the Dutch in order to gain Dutch support against the French. In 1819, the British also took over Singapore which had been under Dutch control.[157]

China fell under British control during the 1800s. Britain wanted to control China for the same economic reason they were interested in South East Asia. The Chinese products the British wanted included silk, porcelain, and tea.[158] The product that the British frequently traded for these Chinese

---

[156] Keat Gin Ooi, *Southeast Asia: A Historical Encyclopedia, from Angkor Wat to East Timor*, Volume 1 (Santa Barbara: ABC CLIO, 2004), 937-938.

[157] Ooi, 937-938.

[158] W. Travis Hanes III, and Frank Sanello *Opium Wars: The Addiction of One Empire and the Corruption of Another* (Naperville: Sourcebooks Inc., 2002), 12, 15.

goods was opium.[159] In order to stop Chinese people from being destroyed by opium addiction, the Chinese government tried to prevent the British from importing opium into China. The British response was war. The first war between Britain and China was, logically, named the First Opium War (1839 to 1842). The war ended in 1842 with Britain as the victor. The war concluded with the Chinese government signing the humiliating Treaty of Nanking.[160] According to the Nanking treaty, China was required to compensate the British for opium that was lost or destroyed during the war. In addition, the treaty granted the British the right to trade at Chinese ports. Finally, Hong Kong was given to the British as a colony.[161] Hong Kong was not returned to China until 1997. From 1856 to 1860, the British and Chinese engaged in a second war called the Second Opium War.[162] This war ended with a series of treaties called the Convention of Peking. The Convention of Peking mandated that China pay the British for engaging in the war. The Convention also required the Chinese to permit the British to ship Chinese people from China to British Colonies. Once these Chinese people arrived in the British colony they were to pay for the cost of the voyage by working for British colonists.[163] Below, are excerpts from the Treaty of Nanking and the Convention of Peking.

---

[159] Hanes and Sanello, 12.

[160] Hanes and Sanello, 13, 154.

[161] "The Treaty of Nanking," Nanking.com, http://www.nanking.com/ (accessed January 31, 2015).

[162] Hanes and Sanello, 3, 175-185.

[163] "1860, Beijing Convention – Britain," China's External Relations – A History, http://www.chinaforeignrelations.net/treaty_beijing (accessed January 31st, 2015).

~ The Treaty of Nanking (1842) ~

Her majesty the Queen of the United Kingdom of Great Britain and Ireland, and His Majesty the Emperor of China, being desirous of putting an end to the misunderstandings and consequent hostilities which have arisen between the two countries, have resolved to conclude a Treaty ...

I. The Government of China having compelled the British merchants trading at Canton to deal exclusively with certain Chinese merchants, called Hong merchants (or Co-Hong), who had been licensed by the Chinese Government for that purpose, the Emperor of China agrees to abolish that practice in future at all ports where British merchants may reside, and to permit them to carry on their mercantile transactions with whatever persons they please... IV. The Emperor of China agrees to pay the sum of 6,000,000 of dollars, as the value of the opium which was delivered up at Canton in the month of March, 1839, as a ransom for the lives of Her Britannic Majesty's Superintendent and subjects, who had been imprisoned and threatened with death by the Chinese High Officers.[164]

~ The Convention of Peking (1860) ~

...Her Majesty the Queen of Great Britain and Ireland, and His Imperial Majesty the Emperor of China, being alike desirous to bring to an end the misunderstanding at present existing between their respective Governments,

---

[164] "The Treaty of Nanking, Nanking.com, http://www.nanking.com (accessed January 13, 2016).

and to secure their relations against further interruption...have agreed upon the following Convention....

Article V.
As soon as the Ratifications of the Treaty of one thousand eight hundred and fifty-eight shall have been exchanged, His Imperial Majesty the Emperor of China, will, by decree, command the high authorities of every province to proclaim throughout their jurisdictions, that Chinese, choosing to take service in the British Colonies or other parts beyond sea, are at perfect liberty to enter into engagements with British Subjects for that purpose, and to ship themselves and their families on board any British vessel at any of the open ports of China. Also that the high authorities aforesaid, shall, in concert with Her Britannic Majesty's Representative in China, frame such regulations for the protection of Chinese emigrating as above, as the circumstances of the different open ports may demand.

Article VI.
With a view to the maintenance of law and order in and about the harbour of Hongkong, His Imperial Majesty the Emperor of China agrees to cede to Her Majesty the Queen of Great Britain and Ireland, and to Her Heirs and Successors, to have and to hold as a dependency of Her Britannic Majesty's Colony of Hongkong, that portion of the township of Cowloon, in the province of Kwangtung, of which a lease was granted in perpetuity to Harry Smith Parkes, Esquire, Companion of the Bath, a Member of the Allied Commission at Canton, on behalf of Her Britannic Majesty's Government, by Lau Tsung Kwang, Governor

General of the Two Kwang.¹⁶⁵

The French in South East Asia

From 111 BC, beginning with the Han Dynasty, to 938 AD Vietnam was ruled by China with two brief interruptions. The first interruption, was from 40-43 when the Trưng sisters revolted against the Chinese, pushed them out of Vietnam and ruled. The second was from 544-602 when for about sixty years Vietnam revolted once more and regained its independence from China. This ended in 602 when China, under the Sui dynasty, once again defeated the Vietnamese and ruled over northern Vietnam. Finally, in 938, Vietnamese troops led by Ngô Quyền (897-944) successfully defeated the Chinese, specifically the Southern Han. Afterwards, Ngô Quyền ruled Vietnam as a king.¹⁶⁶

In the 1400s, Vietnamese autonomy ended once again when the Chinese Ming dynasty invaded and took back Vietnam. The Ming rule over Vietnam lasted only briefly from 1407-1427. In 1427, the Vietnamese rebelled and defeated the Chinese.¹⁶⁷ From 1428 to 1787, Vietnam, known as Dai Viet,¹⁶⁸ was governed by the Le dynasty. Le-Loi was

---

¹⁶⁵ "1860, Beijing Convention – Britain," Chinaforeignrelations.net, http://www.chinaforeignrelations.net/treaty_beijing (accessed January 13, 2016).

¹⁶⁶ K.W. Taylor, *A History of the Vietnamese* (Cambridge: Cambridge University Press, 2013), 17, 21, 35-37, 46.

¹⁶⁷ Taylor, 174-185.

¹⁶⁸ A kingdom now associated with Vietnam was named Dai Co Viet by King Dinh Bo Linh in the 960s AD. When Ly Nhat Ton (r. 1054-1072) became king of the same kingdom, he eliminated the word Co, which in Vietnamese means great, from the title. Not until the twentieth century, was the name Vietnam widely used. K.

the founder of this dynasty. He had successfully led the Vietnamese people to victory against China's Ming dynasty.[169]

The following century, in 1533 according to imperial records of the Le dynasty, a Western priest introduced Christianity in the province of Nam-dinh. Records of the Nguyen, a highly influential family that under the Le vied for power with the Trinh family, state that in 1596 the Spanish Catholic priest Diego Adverte evangelized the Vietnamese in the Quang-nam province.[170] In 1615 and 1626, the Jesuits founded Vietnam's first Catholic Missions. These Jesuits had recently been kicked out of Japan. The Jesuit missions were founded under the supervision of a Portuguese Church overseer. The reason for this was that since 1493, out of respect of Pope Alexander VI's bull *Inter caetera,* missionaries no matter what their country of origin first travelled to Lisbon, Portugal, to give their allegiance to the Portuguese King before going to Asia.[171]

In the 1700s and 1800s, Vietnam was significantly threatened by a foreign power, this time from the Western European world. Prior to the 1700s and 1800s, the Vietnamese had encountered European merchants as far back as the first century AD during the time of the Roman Empire. These early European merchants were interested in trade and not in ruling over Vietnam. This changed when the French, starting in the 1700s, gained greater presence in Vietnam.

W. Taylor, *A History of the Vietnamese* (Cambridge: Cambridge University Press 2013), 72-73, 398.

[169] Mark W. McLeod, *The Vietnamese Response to French Intervention, 1862-1874* (New York: Greenwood Publishing Group, 1991), 1.

[170] McLeod, 3.

[171] McLeod, 4.

In 1787, the French government by signing a treaty supported a militarily intervention in Vietnam. The French signed the treaty in order to heed the advice of a French missionary bishop Pierre Joseph Georges Pigneau. Bishop Pigneau, who was ministering to the Vietnamese, requested France to back Prince Nguyễn Ánh against a rebellion against the Nguyễn Dynasty led by the Tây Sơn brothers of the Binh-dinh province. This rebellion began in 1772. The treaty was signed on November 28, 1787, by the French Foreign minister and by Bishop Pigneau. In it, France promised to aid Prince Nguyễn Ánh in his fight against the rebellion. In exchange, Prince Nguyễn Ánh granted the French exclusive commercial freedom in Vietnam and religious freedom for Catholics in Vietnam. In 1802, Prince Nguyễn Ánh defeated the Tây Sơn rebellion and established himself as Emperor Gia Long.[172]

About fifty years after Prince Nguyen Anh became emperor, France began intensifying its interventions in Vietnam, including militarily. The military advantage of the French caused Vietnam to sign the Treaty of Saigon in 1862. According to the treaty, France was granted land over the region around Saigon. By 1874, French naval officers who had been governing Saigon annexed more land out of which was created the colony of Cochinchina. During the same time, the naval officers also founded a protectorate to govern Cambodia.[173] Similarly, in 1893 France formed a protectorate over Laos. Laos, Cambodia, and Vietnam were all grouped under French rule in 1897 as a Federation of Indochina. A major product that was imported by the French out of Indochina was rubber from rubber-tree plantations. The country that the French focused more attention on adminis-

---

[172] McLeod, 7-10.
[173] McLeod, 446.

tering was Vietnam. While leaving the Cambodian monarchy in place, the French relied upon Vietnamese to administer Cambodia.[174] As a result of French interest in Vietnam, in particular of the South, Vietnam was greatly influenced by French culture to such an extent that its southern central city, Saigon, was known as the "Paris of the Orient." Many South Vietnamese, consequently, assimilated French culture, converted to Catholicism, and spoke French.[175]

The U.S. in Asia

The U.S. presence in Asia became prominent in the mid-1800s. American presence was often accompanied by military force, known as gun boat diplomacy. In 1846, the U.S. practiced hard diplomacy by firing shells from a US ship into Danang of central Vietnam with the intent of motivating the Vietnamese government to release a US missionary who had been spreading Christianity despite being ordered not to.[176] Soft diplomacy was attempted by the U.S. in 1846, when Commodore James Biddle was sent to Japan with two U.S. navy ships in order to establish trade and diplomatic relations. The Japanese officials who received him politely rejected his requests. Biddle then went to China and made the same request to the Chinese who agreed to sign a trade treaty with the U.S. government.[177]

In 1852, the U.S. President Millard Fillmore resorted once again to hard, gunboat diplomacy by sending Commodore Perry with four warships to Japan. They arrived

---

[174] Craig Lockard, *Southeast Asia in World History*, (Oxford: Oxford University Press, 2009), 104, 106-107.

[175] Lockard, 105.

[176] Ebrey, Walthall, and Palais, 298.

[177] Jon Woronoff, *Historical Dictionary of Unites States-Japan Relations* (Plymouth: Scarecrow Press, 2007), 52.

in Japan's Uraga harbor on July 8, 1853. Upon arriving, Perry handed over a letter to Japanese officials.[178] The letter was from the US president and was addressed to the Japanese Emperor. Below are excerpts from this letter:

> ...I have directed Commodore Perry to assure your imperial majesty that I entertain the kindest feelings toward your majesty's person and government, and that I have no other object in sending him to Japan but to propose to your imperial majesty that the United States and Japan should live in friendship and have commercial intercourse with each other.
>
> The Constitution and laws of the United States forbid all interference with the religious or political concerns of other nations. I have particularly charged Commodore Perry to abstain from every act which could possibly disturb the tranquility of your imperial majesty's dominions.
>
> ... I am desirous that our two countries should trade with each other, for the benefit both of Japan and the United States.
>
> We know that the ancient laws of your imperial majesty's government do not allow of foreign trade, except with the Chinese and the Dutch; but as the state of the world changes and new governments are formed, it seems to be wise, from time to time, to make new laws. There was a

---

[178] Asia for Educators, "Letters from U.S. President Millard Fillmore and U.S. Navy Commodore Matthew C. Perry to the Emperor of Japan (1852-1853)," afe.easia.comolubia.edu, http://afe.easia.columbia.edu/ps/japan/fillmore_perry_letters.pdf, (accessed January 19, 2016).

time when the ancient laws of your imperial majesty's government were first made.

...If your imperial majesty is not satisfied that it would be safe altogether to abrogate the ancient laws which forbid foreign trade, they might be suspended for five or ten years, so as to try the experiment. If it does not prove as beneficial as was hoped, the ancient laws can be restored.
...

I have directed Commodore Perry to mention another thing to your imperial majesty. Many of our ships pass every year from California to China; and great numbers of our people pursue the whale fishery near the shores of Japan. It sometimes happens, in stormy weather, that one of our ships is wrecked on your imperial majesty's shores. In all such cases we ask, and expect, that our unfortunate people should be treated with kindness, and that their property should be protected, till we can send a vessel and bring them away. We are very much in earnest in this.

Commodore Perry is also directed by me to represent to your imperial majesty that we understand there is a great abundance of coal and provisions in the Empire of Japan. Our steamships, in crossing the great ocean, burn a great deal of coal, and it is not convenient to bring it all the way from America. We wish that our steamships and other vessels should be allowed to stop in Japan and supply themselves with coal, provisions, and water. They will pay for them in money, or anything else your imperial majesty's subjects may prefer; and we request your imperial majesty to appoint a convenient port, in the southern part of the Empire, where our vessels may stop for this purpose. We are very desirous of this.

These are the only objects for which I have sent Commodore Perry, with a powerful squadron, to pay a visit to your imperial majesty's renowned city of Yedo: friendship, commerce, a supply of coal and provisions, and protection for our shipwrecked people.

...

Your good friend,

MILLARD FILLMORE, President[179]

Along with the above letter, Commodore Perry also delivered his own letter to the Emperor. The letter contains a veiled threat, as is evident below:

... Therefore, as the United States and Japan are becoming every day nearer and nearer to each other, the President desires to live in peace and friendship with your imperial majesty, but no friendship can long exist, unless Japan ceases to act towards Americans as if they her enemies. ... The undersigned holds out all these arguments in the hope that the Japanese government will see the necessity of averting unfriendly collision between the two nations, by responding favorably to the propositions of amity... Many of the large ships-of-war destined to visit Japan have not yet arrived in these seas, though they are hourly expected; and the undersigned, as an evidence of his friendly intentions, has brought but

---

[179] President Filmore, "President Fillmore's letter to the Emperor of Japan, delivered July 14, 1853," us.archive.org., https://ia700804.us.archive.org/27/items/FillmoreLetterToJapanEmperor/Letter_to_Japan_Emperor_nw.txt, (accessed January 19, 2016).

four of the smaller ones, designing, should it become necessary, to return to Edo in the ensuing spring with a much larger force. But it is expected that the government of your imperial majesty will render such return unnecessary, by acceding at once to the very reasonable and pacific overtures contained in the President's letter.
...

M.C. Perry, Commander-in-chief of the United States Naval Forces in the East India, China, and Japan seas[180]

Commodore Perry remained in Uraga, Japan, for about ten days before leaving to the coast of China. Around six months later, he returned to Japan, but this time with six ships armed with more than one hundred canons. The Japanese Tokugawa shogunate, a type of hereditary military general, who was the actual political power and not the Emperor, responded in 1854 by signing the Treaty of Kanagawa, thereby agreeing to the US requests.[181] By agreeing to US demands, the Tokugawa shogunate set the stage for their decline in political power and the rise of a new centralized government in the Meiji Restoration of 1868 with the emperor as the political leader.[182]

---

[180] Asia for Educators, "Letters from Fillmore and Perry to the Emperor of Japan (1852-1853)."

[181] Asia for Educators, "Letters from Fillmore and Perry to the Emperor of Japan (1852-1853)."

[182] Asia for Educators, "Commodore Perry and Japan (1853-1854)," afe.easia.columbia.edu, http://afe.easia.columbia.edu/special/japan_1750_perry.htm (accessed January 19, 2016); U.S. Department of State, Office of the Historian, "The United States and the Opening of Japan, 1853," History.state.gov., https://history.state.gov/milestones/1830-1860/opening-to-japan, (accessed January 19, 2016).

Perry, the U.S. President and many Americans were influenced by a number of factors that helped cause them to be convinced that their gunboat diplomacy with the Japanese was justified. These factors include philosophical, economic, political, and religious motivations. Philosophically, the U.S. believed in a general idea called Manifest Destiny. The historian William Earl Weeks identifies three central themes that repeatedly are stressed in the various expressions of Manifest Destiny. They are "the special virtues of the American people and their institutions; their mission to redeem and remake the world in the image of America; and the American destiny under God to accomplish this sublime task."[183] The economic and political motivations included the desire to expand U.S. trade relations and to protect the American whaling industry that needed supply states and safe harbors when Americans were shipwrecked. The religious motivation was promoted mainly by Protestant missionaries who believed they had a divine calling to spread the gospel in Asia.[184]

In contrasting the style of evangelization in Asia by Jesuit priests with the U.S. Protestant missionary style the scholars of *East Asia: A Cultural, Political and Social History* state:

> In contrast to priests who first spread Catholicism around the globe, nineteenth-century missionaries who likewise took the world as their stage were often nondenominational and as likely to be female as male. Unlike the

---

[183] William Earl Weeks, *Building the Continental Empire: American Expansion from the Revolution to the Civil War* (Chicago: Ivan R. Dee, 1996), 61.

[184] U.S. Department of State, Office of the Historian, "The United States and the Opening of Japan, 1853," History.state.gov., https://history.state.gov/milestones/1830-1860/opening-to-japan, (accessed January 19, 2016).

Jesuits, who had tried to conciliate power holders and adjust to local practices, missionaries from Britain and the United States had a vision of Christianity that admitted no compromise with what they deemed heathen practices and beliefs. Impatient at restrictions on their activities imposed by treaties, they caused more than one international incident.[185]

~ Artistic Representation of the U.S. Manifest Destiny ~

186

---

[185] Ebrey, Walthall, and Palais, 299.

[186] John Gast, "*American Progress*, an 1872 painting by John Gast is an allegorical representation of the modernization of the new west. Here Columbia, a personification of the United States, leads civilization westward with American settlers. She brings light from the East into the darkness of the West, stringing telegraph wire as she sweeps west; she holds a school book as well (it is not a Bible). The different stages of economic activity of the pioneers are highlighted and, especially, the evolving forms of transportation."

The Russians in Asia

Shortly after the U.S. was establishing its presence in Asia, Russia in the 1890s intensified their efforts to gain control in Asia. The Japanese defeat of the Chinese in the First Sino-Japanese War (1894-1895) motivated the Russians to reach into China in order to push out Japanese presence which the Russians feared were threatening Russian power. According to the Treaty of Shimonoseki, signed between representatives of Japan and China in 1895, China agreed to recognize the autonomy of Korea, China agreed to give to Japan Taiwan (formerly Formosa) and a number of islands by Taiwan, and China agreed to give to Japan the eastern portion of the Liaodong Peninsula bay.[187]

To contain Japan's thrust into China, Russia, backed by Germany and France, convinced Japan to give up its claim over the Liaodong Peninsula Bay under the condition that China would pay for the loss of the bay with the help of a Russian loan. Later, in 1896, Russia signed a Li-Lobanov treaty in which Russia pledged to defend China's territory against further incursions by foreign powers. Russia also obtained a lease from China over the Liaodong Peninsula which enabled them to build a naval base called Port Arthur. Other agreements beneficial to Russia were also obtained from China.[188]

---

scan or photograph of 1872 painting, https://commons.wikimedia.org/wiki/File%3AAmerican_progress.JPG (accessed January 19, 2016).

[187] "Treaty of Shimonoseki," Signed at Shimonoseki 17 April, 1895,Taiwan Documents Project, http://www.taiwanbasic.com/treaties/Shimonoseki.htm (accessed January 21, 2016).

[188] H. Rogger, *Russia in the Age of Modernisation and Revolution 1881-1917* (London: Routledge, 1983), 176.

Quiz 7

1. (12 points) Compare and contrast British, French, Russian, and U.S. presence in East Asia during the 1800s and 1900s. Include in your answer the following: Crimean War, Opium Wars, Treaty of Nanking and the Convention of Peking, Bishop Pigneau and the treaty he encouraged, Indochina, Saigon, Commodore Perry, gun boats, Manifest Destiny, First Sino-Japanese War.

2. (Two points) How did Commodore Perry threaten the Japanese in his letter of 1853 addressed to the Japanese Emperor?

3. (Two points) What is Manifest Destiny and how did this philosophy influence the U.S. East Asian foreign relations during the 1800s-1900s?

4. (Two points) Compare and contrast the style of evangelization in Asia done by Jesuit priests with that done by U.S. Protestants in Asia.

Chapter 8: East Asian Nationalism

Introduction

East Asian countries responded to Western imperialism with nationalism. In order to understand what nationalism is, the terms nation and state need to be defined. A state, in the sense of a politically sovereign state, refers to a defined territory that is ruled by a government with the power to legislate, enforce, and judge laws. A nation is comprised of a group of people who share significant characteristics. These characteristics may include ethnic, religious, linguistic, and historical components. A nation-state is a self-governing political entity that is united by a dominant national identity. According to this definition, not all sovereign states are nation-states because it is possible to have multiple nations within a sovereign state. Such a state is a polyglot state and is made up by a number of large national groups. The former Yugoslavia was a polyglot state, which was a factor in its demise. In contrast, the Palestinians are a stateless nation since they have no land of their own and yet are a people. As a further contrast, the Cherokee Indian tribe is a nation with land of its own within the U.S.[189]

---

[189] For a more detailed explanation of these terms see Thomas M. Magstadt, *Understanding Politics: Ideas, Institutions and Issues Tenth Edition*, Belmont: Cengage Learning 2013, 6-9.

Now that terms directly related in our linguistic ecosystem to nationalism have been defined, we will define nationalism. According to nationalism, every nation has a right to be an autonomous political entity. In other words, for every nation there ought to be a state.[190] This common assumption is a relatively new one in world history. Antiquity and the medieval times had empires and kingdoms in which nations co-existed. Nationalism first developed after Europe's medieval time. After the American Revolution (1775-1783) and the French Revolution (1789-1799) nationalism intensified, and spread across Europe bringing in its wake a series of wars in which nationalities fought for their independence. About a century later, in the late 1800s, nationalism arose in East and South East Asia. According to the basic principle of nationalism that for every nation there ought to be a sovereign state, Asians began to rebel against colonial and imperial rule. As a result, nationalistic movements became prominent in China, Japan, Korea, Indonesia, Vietnam, Burma, and to a lesser extent in Cambodia, Laos, Malaya stop, and the Philippines.

China and the Boxer Rebellion

About forty years after the Second Opium War (1856-1860) and during the summer of 1898, China's Shandong province experienced a terrible flood. The flood was caused by the breaking of Yellow River dikes. Millions of Chinese quickly became homeless, and crops were destroyed. Some people expressed their frustration by directing their anger at

---

[190] This is a reference to Ernest Gellner's definition of nationalism. Lawrence Cahoone, *The Modern Political Tradition: Hobbes to Habermas*, Lectures 1-18 (Chantilly: The Great Courses, 2014), 211.

the government and at foreigners, specifically foreign missionaries. The movement that gradually took place was called by Westerners "Boxers" because of the ability of some in the anti-government and anti-foreigner movement to box, or to practice martial arts. In 1899, the governor of the Shandong province was able to put an end to the civil unrest caused by the Boxers. The Boxers responded by moving to other regions in China where they intensified their rhetoric by demanding death to foreigners in China and to Chinese who had become corrupted by foreign influence.

On June 20th, 1900, the German minister Baron von Kettler was assassinated in Beijing. Following the incident, foreigners took refuge in the well-built North Cathedral of Beijing of the Legation Quarter. According to eyewitness accounts, the Boxers vented their anger against foreigners and Chinese suspected of being foreign collaborators in the following manner:

> Women and children hacked to pieces, men trussed like fowls, with noses and ears cut off and eyes gouged out. ... Many were found roasted alive, and so massacred and cut up as to be unrecognizable... the stench of human blood in the hot June air was almost intolerable, and the signs more than we could bear. Men, women, and children lay indiscriminately heaped together, some hacked to pieces, other with their throats cut from ear to ear, some still moving, others quite motionless. ... their fiendish murderers were at their incantations burning incense before their gods, offering Christians in sacrifice to their angered deities.[191]

---

[191] Diana Preston, *The Boxer Rebellion: The Dramatic Story of China's War on Foreigners That Shook the word in the Summer of 1900* (New York: Walker & Company, 2000), 76.

With the support of Japan, Western countries responded by sending in twenty thousand troops. Within a year's time, there was a forty-five thousand eight-nation force in northern China. These troops brought an end to the Boxer revolt.[192] On September 7, 1901, the Qing Empire of China signed a multilateral treaty called Boxer Protocol. The other sides represented included Germany, Austro-Hungary, Belgium, Spain, the U.S., France, Great Britain, Italy, Japan, Holland, and Russia. Below are a few excerpts from the treaty:

Article I.
...
(*b.*) The Chinese Government has announced that it will erect, on the spot of the murder of His Excellency Baron von Ketteler, a Memorial Monument corresponding to the rank of the deceased, with an inscription in Latin, German, and Chinese, which shall express the regret of His Majesty the Emperor of China for the murder done.
...
Article II.
(*a.*) Imperial Edicts of the 13th and 21st February, 1901 (Annexes 4, 5 and 6), pronounced the following punishments upon the chief culprits for the attacks and crimes which took place against the friendly Governments and their subjects:
...
(*b.*) An Imperial Edict promulgated on the 19th August, 1901 (Annex 8), has ordered the suspension of

---

[192] Patricia Ebrey, Anne Walthall, and James Palais, *East Asia: A Cultural, Social, and Political History* (Belmont: Wadsworth, 2009), 320-321; Preston, 43, 81-82.

the official examinations during five years, in all towns where foreigners were murdered or were subjected to harsh treatment

Article III.

In order to make suitable amends for the murder of Mr. Sugiyama, Chancellor of the Japanese Legation, His Majesty the Emperor of China, by an Imperial Edict of 18th June, 1901 (Annex 9), has appointed the Vice-President of the Ministry of Finance, Na T'ung, an Extraordinary Ambassador, and specially commanded him to convey to His Majesty the Emperor of Japan the expression of the regret of His Majesty the Emperor of China and His Government for the murder of Mr. Sugiyama.

Article IV.

The Chinese Government has agreed to erect an expiatory monument in each of the foreign or international cemeteries which has been desecrated or in which grave monuments have been destroyed.

...

Article V.

China has agreed to forbid the import into its territory of arms and ammunition, as well as of all material exclusively employed for the manufacture of arms and ammunition.

An Imperial Edict has been issued on 25th August, 1901 (Annex 11), forbidding such importation for two years.

Further Edicts may be promulgated in the future in order to extend this period every two years, in case the Powers deem it necessary.

Article VI.

In an Imperial Edict of 22nd May, 1901 (Annex 12), His Majesty the Emperor of China has agreed to pay the Powers an indemnity of 450 million Haikuan taels. This sum represents the total of the indemnity for the States, companies or societies, individuals and Chinese which are mentioned in Article VI of the note of 22nd December, 1900.

(*a.*) These 450 million taels constitute a debt in gold for which the rate of the Haikuan tael is calculated in the gold currency of each country in the following manner: ...[193]

Japan and the Fall of the Shogunate

The previous chapter presented Commodore Perry's hard diplomacy with Japan and the Shogunate's capitulations to his demands by signing the 1854 Treaty of Kanagawa. In 1858, the first U.S. consul to Japan, Townsend Harris, negotiated a commercial treaty with Japan that exceeded the Treaty of Kanagawa. A few excerpts from the Harris Treaty or Treaty of Amity and Commerce are below:

Treaty between the United States of America and the Japanese Empire.

The President of the United States of America, and his Majesty the Tycoon of Japan, desiring to establish on firm and lasting foundations the relations of peace and friendship now happily existing between the two coun-

---

[193] "1901, Boxer Protocol – Multilateral," chinaforeignrelations.net, http://chinaforeignrelations.net/node/185 (accessed January 26, 2016).

tries, and to secure the best interest of their respective citizens and subjects, by encouraging, facilitating, and regulating their industry and trade, have resolved to conclude a treaty of amity and commerce for this purpose ....

I.
There shall henceforward be perpetual peace and friendship between the United States of America and his Majesty the Tycoon of Japan, and his successors.

The President of the United States may appoint a diplomatic agent to reside at the city of Yedo, and consuls or consular agents to reside at any or all of the ports in Japan which are opened for American commerce by this treaty. The diplomatic agent and consul-general of the United States, shall have the right to travel freely in any part of the empire of Japan, from the time they enter on the discharge of their official duties.
...
III.
In addition to the ports of Simoda and Hafcodade, the following ports and towns shall be opened on the dates respectively appended to them, that is to say: — Kanagawa on the (4th of July, 1859,) .... Nagasaki on the (4th of July 1859,) .... Nee-e-gata on the (1st of January, 1860,) .... Hiogo on the (1st of January, 1863,) ....
...
IV.
The importation of opium is prohibited ... No higher duties shall be paid by Americans on goods imported into Japan, than are fixed by this treaty, nor shall any higher duties be paid by Americans than are levied on the same description of goods if imported in Japanese vessels, or

the vessels of any other nation.

VII.
In the opened harbors of Japan, Americans shall be free to go where they please, within the following limits: ...

VIII.
Americans in Japan shall be allowed the free exercise of their religion, and for this purpose shall have the right to erect suitable places of worship. No injury shall be done to such buildings, nor any insult be offered to the religious worship of the Americans. American citizens shall not injure any Japanese temple or mia, or offer any insult or injury to Japanese religious ceremonies, or to the objects of their worship.[194]

When Emperor Komei (reigned 1846-1867) was asked to support the shogunate's signing the Harris treaty he refused and even, in May of 1863, formally demanded that the U.S. and other foreign presence be expelled from Japan. The emperor's nationalism was supported by many who viewed the shogunate as having committed an act of treason by signing the Harris treaty. Tension naturally developed between supporters of the shogunate and supporters of the emperor. When Emperor Komei died in 1867, he was succeeded by Emperor Meiji (reigned 1867-1912). Meiji, who share Komei's anti-western beliefs, had the office of the shogun terminated. The shogunate responded by fighting the emperor's forces. In four days, the shogunate's forces were

---

[194] "Treaty between the United States of America and the Japanese Empire," Signed July 29, 1858, archive.org., https://archive.org/stream/treatiesandconvoounkngoog/treatiesandconvoounkngoog_djvu.txt, (accessed January 26, 2016).

defeated and Emperor Meiji was able to firmly establish his power.[195]

Korea and Isolationism

Like Japan, Korea also responded to Western power with nationalism. Under the reign of Prince Heungseon, Korea isolated itself from foreign powers. Prince Heungseon ruled Korea (1864-1874) since the Joseon dynasty, which had ruled Korea with 25 successive kings, did not have an heir. This led the queen dowager to choose an heir. She chose Prince Heungseon's son as the heir, but since the prince's son was only eleven years old, Prince Heungseon ruled in his son's place until his son was mature enough to rule. Upon taking the throne, Prince Heungseon took the title Grand Prince, or Daewongun. Under his rule, he consistently rejected Western invitations to enter into a commercial relationship, even when these overtures were made with Western warships. In one case, the USS General Sherman, an American merchant ship, was burned and its crew killed when this ship, armed with cannons, entered into Korea's Daedong River.[196]

When Daewongun's son Gojong came of age, he took the throne as King Gojong (reigned 1864-1907). King Gojong changed Korea's direction by reforming the monarchy and opening up Korea to foreign trade. At first, though, when Meiji Japan sent a letter to the Korean court requesting in strong language a trading agreement, King Gojong, listening to his advisors, rejected it. This caused Meiji Japan to imitate the Western practice of gunboat diplomacy. On September

---

[195] Ebrey, Walthall, and Palais, 330-336.
[196] Djun Kil Kim, *The History of Korea*, 2nd Edition (Santa Barbara: ABC-CLIO, LLC, 2014), 118-122.

20, 1875, a Japanese warship entered into Korean waters, and engaged in a battle with the Korean military. This military conflict between Korea and Japan ended with Japan as the victor and Korea signing for the first time a modern treaty with a foreign power, the 1876 Ganghwa Treaty, signed by King Gojong. King Gojong signed this treaty despite resistance from influential governmental officials urging him not to.[197]

The Japanese victory encouraged other foreign powers to also establish trade agreements with Korea. In order to reduce Japanese influence over Korea, China's Qing dynasty solidified its economic relationship with Korea. On May 22, 1882, the United States became the first Western country to establish a trade agreement with Korea called the Treaty of Peace, Amity, Commerce and Navigation. In 1883, Britain and Germany signed trade treaties with Korea. This was followed by Russia signing a trade treaty with Korea in 1884. Finally, France, signed a treaty with Korea in 1886. France's treaty included an article that allowed Catholic missionaries to evangelize in Korea.

During the 1880s, supporters of Daewongun's isolationist policy demanded he replace his son as king. This caused riots and political unrest that troubled both China and Japan. They responded by sending troops to Korea in support of King Gojong. Daewongun was captured by the Chinese and taken into China. With his father out of the way, King Gojong renewed his open door policy with the slogan "Eastern way and Western technology."[198] In 1897, after persevering through political turmoil, including the failed Gapsin Coup of 1884, King Gojong greatly won over public approval proclaiming Korea an Empire. This act signaled that Korea was

---

[197] Kim, 123-124.
[198] Kim, 127.

independent from and equal in status to China and other countries. His empire and rule came to an end when Japan, after successfully defeating Russia in the Russo-Japanese War (1904-1905), forced Emperor Gojong to abdicate, and in 1910 annexed Korea under the Japan-Korea Annexation Treaty.[199]

South East Asian Colonies and Nationalism

In varying degrees, nationalism also arose throughout South East Asia. Since it would be to lengthy to compare and contrast the various expressions of nationalism in South East Asia during the time frame we are studying, I will conclude with a poetic expression of nationalism, called the *Tale of Kieu*, from Vietnam. The poem *The Tale of Kieu*, written by Nguyen Du in the early 1800s, represents the hidden nationalistic spirit of the Vietnamese during the 1800s. The poem tells the story of a beautiful, intelligent young woman Kieu. Although she was forced into concubinage and later into prostitution, she remained true to the one she truly loved. By so doing, in the eyes of the Vietnamese, she retained her dignity and honor. Kieu was understood at the time to symbolize the Vietnamese people who kept their honor even though they were forced into servitude both by the French Imperialists and Vietnamese who collaborated with the French.[200] Below is an excerpt of from *The Tale of Kieu*.

"An oath bound us together," he replied. We split, like fish to sea and bird to sky. Through your long exile how I grieved for you! Breaking your troth, you must have

---

[199] Kim, xxi, 134-146.
[200] Craig Lockard, *Southeast Asia in World History*, (Oxford: Oxford University Press, 2009), 102.

suffered so. We loved each other, risked our lives. Braved death now we two meet again, still deep in love. The willow in mid-spring still has green leaves I thought you still attached to human love. But no more dust stains your clear mirror now; your vow can't but increase my high regard. If I long searched the sea for my lost pin, it was true love, not lust, that urged me on. We're back together now, beneath one roof; to live in concord, need two share one bed?"

Kieu pinned her hair and straightened up her gown, then knelt to touch her head in gratitude: "If ever my soiled body's cleansed of stains, I'll thank a gentleman, a noble soul. The words you spoke came from a kindred heart: no true empathy between two souls. A home, a refuge – what won't you give me? My honor loves again as of tonight."[201]

Quiz 8

1. (Three Points) Define nationalism. Include the following terms in your definition: nation, state, and the basic principle of nationalism.

2. (Four Points) Why do you think the violent nationalism of the Boxer Rebellion occurred and how did this rebellion end? In responding include the following: Opium Wars, flood, Boxers, Boxer Protocol.

---

[201] Nguyễn Du, *The Tale of Kieu: A Bilingual Edition of Truyen Kieu*, trans. Huynh Sanh Thong (New Haven: Yale University Press, 1983), verses 3165-3186, p. 163.

3. (Five Points) Discuss the different expressions of nationalism in Japan. Include in your answer Commodore Perry, gun boat diplomacy, Townsend Harris, the shogunate, and emperor Komei.

4. (Five Points) Compare and contrast Daewongun's and his son Gojong's response to foreign power. Include the following in your response: identify who Daewongun and Gojong were, USS General Sherman, Ganghwa Treaty, open door policy of Gojong.

5. (Five Points) Interpret the following excerpt from *The Tale of Kieu* from the perspective of nationalism.

"An oath bound us together," he replied. We split, like fish to sea and bird to sky. Through your long exile how I grieved for you! Breaking your troth, you must have suffered so. We loved each other, risked our lives. Braved death now we two meet again, still deep in love. The willow in mid-spring still has green leaves I thought you still attached to human love. But no more dust stains your clear mirror now; your vow can't but increase my high regard. If I long searched the sea for my lost pin, it was true love, not lust, that urged me on. We're back together now, beneath one roof; to live in concord, need two share one bed?"

Kieu pinned her hair and straightened up her gown, then knelt to touch her head in gratitude: "If ever my soiled body's cleansed of stains, I'll thank a gentleman, a noble soul. The words you spoke came from a kindred heart: no true empathy between two souls. A home, a refuge – what won't you give me? My honor loves again as of tonight."[202]

---

[202] Du, verses 3165-3186, p. 163.

Chapter 9: East Asia and the West – Rejection, Assimilation, Transformation

Introduction

East and South East Asian countries responded to Western imperialism with nationalism, as described in the previous chapter, and in a variety of other ways including assimilating certain aspects of Western civilization, and rejecting others. In the midst of this process, Asian cultures were transformed while retaining their uniquely eastern characteristics. In studying this transformation, we will focus our attention on a few Asian countries beginning with Korea before examining China, Japan, Indonesia, Burma, and Vietnam.

Korea's Response to Western Culture

Chapter eight contrasted the isolationist policy of Daewongun (reigned 1864-1874) with the open door policy of his son Gojong (1864-1907), who became Korea's first emperor. During the reigns of both Daewongun and his son, Christianity was severely persecuted. According to a Korean textbook from this time, the reason was mainly due to many Christian missionaries rejecting the Asian, Confucian influenced practice of ancestor worship, as is evident below:

> In the opinion of the new generation the so-called Christian religion of the Europeans is mean, superficial and wrong, and is an example of the viciousness of barbarian customs which is not worthy of being studied seriously. The terms used by Christians for heaven, happiness and misfortune are similar to those used by the Buddhists. They worship the heavenly spirits, but not their ancestors. They insult heaven in many ways and confuse the social system. This is really characteristic of barbarian ruthlessness and not worth to be dealt with in our survey of foreign customs. This is especially true since this religion is in a state of decay at present. Europeans have spread their spawn in all countries in the world except China. Everybody adores this religion. We are surprised to see that Chinese scholars and the Chinese people did not avoid the infection.[203]

From 1785 to 1886, Korean Catholicism was suppressed in a series of waves. Among these waves of persecution were the Sinhae, Sinyu, the Kihae, the Pyongo, and Pyongin Persecution. The Sinyu persecution of 1801 was the first nation-wide persecution in Korea. During 1801, Western learning, including religious education, was prohibited. The Kihae Persecution began in 1839 and lasted about a year. It claimed about two hundred martyrs. The Pyongo Persecution of 1846 involved the first Korean-born Catholic priest Fr. Andrew Kim Tae-gon.

Fr. Kim Tae-gon was ordained in Shanghai, China, as Korea's first Catholic priest. He returned to his home country

---

[203] Jurgen Kleiner, *Korea, a Century of Change* (Boston: World Scientific, 2001), 6-7.

in 1845. While in his home country, he was arrested and sentenced to execution by hanging. The Pyongin Persecution began in 1866 when King Gojong issued a Reject Heresy Pronouncement that specifically targeted Catholics. The pronouncement described Catholicism as undermining national unity and requested Koreans who were Catholics to abandon the Catholic faith and embrace Confucianism instead. It is roughly estimated that between eight thousand to twenty thousand Christians were martyred during this persecution.[204] In 1886, the nearly century-long intense persecution of Catholics in Korea ended, except for a few outbursts, when Korea and France signed a Treaty which contained an article that allowed Catholic missionaries to come to Korea.[205] Below is an excerpt from Pope St. John Paul II's homily for the canonization mass of one hundred and three Korean martyrs held in Seoul, Korea, May 6th, 1984:

> The truth about Jesus Christ also reached Korean soil. It came by means of books brought from China. And in a most marvelous way, divine grace soon moved your scholarly ancestors first to an intellectual quest for the truth of God's word and then to a living faith in the Risen Savior.
>
> Yearning for an ever greater share in the Christian faith, your ancestors sent one of their own in 1784 to Peking,

---

[204] Jai-Keun Choi, *The Origin of the Roman Catholic Church in Korea: An Examination of Popular and Governmental Responses to Catholic Missions in the Latin Choson Dynasty* (Cheltenham: The Hermit Kingdom Press, 2006), 1, 188-189, 190 217-218, 325, 330.

[205] Djun Kil Kim, *The History of Korea*, 2nd Edition (Santa Barbara: ABC-CLIO, LLC, 2014), 125.

where he was baptized. From this good seed was born the first Christian community in Korea, a community unique in the history of the Church by reason of the fact that it was founded entirely by lay people. This fledgling Church, so young and yet so strong in faith, withstood wave after wave of fierce persecution. Thus, in less than a century, it could already boast of some ten thousand martyrs. The years 1791, 1801, 1827, 1839, 1846 and 1866 are forever signed with the holy blood of your Martyrs and engraved in your hearts.

Even though the Christians in the first half century had only two priests from China to assist them, and these only for a time, they deepened their unity in Christ through prayer and fraternal love; they disregarded social classes and encouraged religious vocations. And they sought ever closer union with their Bishop in Peking and the Pope in faraway Rome.

After years of pleading for more priests to be sent, your Christian ancestors welcomed the first French missionaries in 1836. Some of these, too, are numbered among the Martyrs who gave their lives for the sake of the Gospel, and who are being canonized today in this historic celebration.

The splendid flowering of the Church in Korea today is indeed the fruit of the heroic witness of the Martyrs. Even today, their undying spirit sustains the Christians in the Church of silence in the North of this tragically divided land.

...

Listen to the last words of Teresa Kwon, one of the early Martyrs: "Since the Lord of Heaven is the Father of all

mankind and the Lord of all creation, how can you ask me to betray him? Even in this world anyone who betrays his own father or mother will not be forgiven. All the more may I never betray him who is the Father of us all".
A generation later, Peter Yu's father Augustine firmly declares: "Once having known God, I cannot possibly betray him". Peter Cho goes even further and says: "Even supposing that one's own father committed a crime, still one cannot disown him as no longer being one's father. How then can I say that I do not know the heavenly Lord Father who is so good?"

And what did the seventeen-year-old Agatha Yi say when she and her younger brother were falsely told that their parents had betrayed the faith? "Whether my parents betrayed or not is their affair. As for us, we cannot betray the Lord of heaven whom we have always served." Hearing this, six other adult Christians freely delivered themselves to the magistrate to be martyred. Agatha, her parents and those other six are all being canonized today. In addition, there are countless other unknown, humble martyrs who no less faithfully and bravely served the Lord.

...

May this solemn day become a pledge of life and of holiness for future generations. Jesus Christ has risen from the dead and is living in his Church today. "Yes it is true. The Lord has risen". Amen. Alleluia![206]

---

[206] John Paul II, "Mass for the Canonization of Korean Martyrs, Homily of Pope John Paul II," Youido Place – Seoul, Sunday, 6 May 1984, w2.vatican.va, http://w2.vatican.va/content/john-paul-ii/en/homilies/1984/documents/hf_jp-ii_hom_19840506_martiri-coreani.html (accessed February 9, 2016).

Near the end of the Christian persecution, a peasant revolt arose that, after a series of steps, led to a governmental policy for all Koreans to embrace a Western-formed modern outlook. The peasant revolt took place in 1894 and was led mainly by peasants upset with the government. After the revolt defeated governmental forces a number of times, King Gojong appealed to China for aid. China agreed and sent aid but, contrary to an agreement it signed with Japan in the 1885 Convention of Tientsin, failed to inform the Japanese. According to the Convention of Tientsin, China and Japan were to inform each other in writing if one of them sent troops into Korea. Japan took this slight to begin a war with China, the first Sino-Japanese War (1894-1895), defeated China, and then replaced China's role as the dominant power in East Asia, in particular over Korea.[207]

With Korea now under its control, Japan insisted King Gojong institute a reform movement called the Kabo reform led by the Japanese influenced Korean Kabo cabinet. According to the Kabo reform, Korea was to reject traditional ways and modernize. Following the cabinet's request, King Gojong supported this movement, which included issuing a decree that mandated all Korean men cut off their traditional topknots. This decree and other aspects of the reform movement was met with such great resistance that King Gojong allied himself with Russia, dismissed the Kabo cabinet, and then in 1897 declared Korea an empire. The decree signified that Korea was independent from both China and Japan.[208] Japan would later defeat Russia in the Russo-Japanese War (1904-1905). Afterwards, Japan forced

---

[207] Patricia Ebrey, Anne Walthall, and James Palais, *East Asia: A Cultural, Social, and Political History* (Belmont: Wadsworth, 2009), 365-368; Kleiner, 17.

[208] Ebrey, Walthall, and Palais, 365-368; Kleiner, 21-22.

Emperor Gojong to abdicate, and in 1910 annexed Korea with the Japan-Korea Annexation Treaty.[209]

China's Response to Western Culture

In the 1800s, many Chinese responded to Western Culture by striving to assimilate various Western features. One interesting, and tragic, way this assimilation occurred was in respect to Christianity introduced into China by Westerners. In 1836, while in his twenties preparing for the second stage of civil service Confucian examinations in the city of Guangzhou (Canton), Hong Xiuquan (1814-1864) was introduced to Christianity by the American Protestant Reverend Edwin Stevens. After failing the second stage of civil service exams, Hong tried once again to pass them in the following year, 1837, but also failed. Soon after his second failure he became very sick, and while recovering claimed he experienced a series of mystical visions involving an old man, representing his father, a younger man, representing his older brother, a woman, representing his mother, and demons. A number of years later, he interpreted the old man as representing God, the woman, as Mary, the younger man as Jesus Christ, and the demons as the Manchu rulers of China's Qing Dynasty.[210]

He also interpreted his visions as signifying that he was Jesus's younger brother and, consequently, a son of God. Convinced that he was the younger brother of Jesus and a son of God, Hong Xiuquan began preaching his own, Chinese

---

[209] Kim, xxi, 134-146.

[210] Jonathan D. Spence, *God's Chinese Son: Heavenly Kingdom of Hong Xiuquan* (New York: Norton & Company, 1996), xxi, 11, 23, 46-50; Odd Arne Westad, *Restless Empire: China and the World Since 1750* (New York: Basic Books, 2012), 47-49.

influenced version of certain Christian teachings. The moral teaching of Xiuquan's religion forbade opium smoking, prostitution, slavery, gambling, polygamy, wine, and tobacco use.[211] By 1850, Hong Xiuquan had attracted thousands of followers. The rapid growth of this religious sect so greatly disturbed the Chinese government that they attempted to arrest Hong, but unsuccessfully. Meanwhile, Hong organized around 20,000 men and women into an army which advanced against the Chinese government with the intention of overthrowing the Manchus and establishing Hong and his "elder brother Jesus" as the rulers over China. In 1851, Hong proclaimed he was founding a "Christian" state in China called the Heavenly Kingdom of Great Peace. From 1851 to 1864, Hong's religious forces fought the Chinese government's forces in what is now called the Taiping Civil War. The estimated dead from the war was in the tens of millions.[212]

During the Taiping Civil War, a scholar named Feng Guifen admiringly observed how effectively Western forces in the ceded territory of Shanghai fought against the radical religious rebels. This admiration came out in one of his essays.[213] In describing Feng's discriminating appreciation of Western ways, Jonathan D. Spence states:

> Feng argued that China must learn to "strengthen itself" ... by including foreign languages, mathematics, and science in the curriculum: Chinese students excelling in

---

[211] Hong Beom Rhee, *Asian Millenarianism: An Interdisciplinary Study of the Taiping and Tonghak Rebellions in a Global Context* (New York: Cambria Press, 2007), 237.

[212] Spence, *God's Chinese Son*, xxi, 11, 23, 46-50; Westad, 47-49.

[213] Ebrey, Walthall, and Palais, 313; Zhu Weizheng, *Rereading Chinese History*, trans. Michael Dillon (Leiden: Brill, 2015), 288.

these subjects should be granted the provincial examination degree. China was a hundred times larger than France and two hundred times larger than England. Feng wrote, so "why are they small and yet so strong? Why are we large and yet weak?" The answer lay in the greater skills of foreigners in four main areas: utilizing all their manpower resources, exploiting their soil to the full, maintaining close bonds between ruler and subjects, and ensuring "the necessary accord of word with deed." In order to start building China's strength, Feng argued, "what we then have to learn from the barbarians is only one thing, solid ships and effective guns." This could be achieved by establishing shipyards and arsenals in selected ports, and by hiring foreign advisers to train Chinese intelligence and wisdom of the Chinese are necessarily superior to those of the various barbarians," the conclusion was clear: China would first learn from foreigners, then equal them, and finally surpass them.[214]

Feng Guifen's praise of Western technology was seconded by a number of other influential scholars, officials, and political figures, in particular Li Hongzhang who as governor-general of Zhili province actively promoted a western form of industrialization and modernization of the Chinese military. Even though what was being promoted was mainly Western science and Western technology, other scholars, officials and political leaders rejected this emulation of the West. The de facto ruler of China at the time, Empress Dowager Cixi carefully avoided taking sides and instead played the various sides off one another. In 1911, a few years after her death, the Qing Dynasty was

---

[214] Jonathan D. Spence, *The Search for Modern China* (New York: Norton & Company Ltd., 1990), 197.

overthrown and replaced by about a decade long period of competing warlords. In the 1920s, the warlords lost their power when the Nationalist Sun Yatsen with his Nationalist Party and military force unified the country once again. The question, though, of what was the proper way to approach Western ways remained unresolved.[215]

Japan's Response to Western Culture

In 1825, Japan's shogunate officially closed its ports to the West. The reasons were both economic and religious. It was feared that the introduction of Christianity into Japan would threaten Japan's national identity by weakening its Confucian-based social structure. It was also feared that Western countries were intent on establishing trade relations that would be disadvantageous to Japan. A few decades later, as was explained in chapter seven, the U.S. with its gunboat diplomacy persuaded Japan's shogunate to open Japan's ports to trade. As a result, the shogunate declined in public approval while the emperor rose in public favor. Taking advantage of this unpopularity of the shogunate, the emperor and his forces restored Japan's monarchy to actual power. In the process, supporters of greater interaction with Western ways lost their influence and in some cases were even killed.[216]

The scholar Sakuma Shozan was one such scholar who was murdered.[217] The following poem by Sakuma's Shozan succinctly captures his pro-Western view:

---

[215] Ebrey, Walthall, and Palais, 401-405.
[216] Ebrey, Walthall, and Palais, 330-331.
[217] Ebrey, Walthall, and Palais, 332.

Eastern ethics and Western science
Complete a circular pattern
Just as two semi-circular molds form one mold
The width of the Earth is 10,000 ri
One half of it should not be missing.[218]

The "Eastern ethics" Sakuma was referring to is Confucian-based. The "Western science" he was referring to was specified by Sakuma as follows:

> In the present world, the traditional knowledge of Japan and China is not sufficient. It is necessary to study the way of governing and managing in the five continents. Considering general world conditions, after the three great discoveries-that is, Columbus's discovery of the new world, assisted by scientific navigation; Copernicus's discovery of the true principles of the motion of the Earth; and Newton's discovery of the true principles of gravitation-the foundation of all the sciences have been firmly established and have become accurate, without any evidence of superstitious beliefs. Owing to these discoveries, conditions in Europe and the United States have generally shown a remarkable improvement. Steamships, magnetism and telegraphs have all been invented.[219]

Even though the emperor-led Meiji Japan had successfully risen to power by rejecting Western influence under Meiji rule, western ideas and practices were still assimilated

---

[218] This poem, titled *Seikenroku*, was written by Sakuma to a student of his. John E. Van Sant, "Sakuma Shozan's Hegelian Vision for Japan," *Asian Philosophy* 14, no. 3 (2004), 281.

[219] John E. Van Sant, "Sakuma Shozan's Hegelian Vision for Japan," *Asian Philosophy* 14, no. 3 (2004), 284.

and even encouraged. For example, in order to strengthen its people, the Meiji government encouraged eating more meat, western vegetables, and fruit. Westerners were also hired to modernize Japanese business practices, education, and legal codes, to name a few. The Japanese people also responded by not only eating certain Western foods but also by wearing Western clothing and appearances. Military uniforms began to replace Samurai attire. Women, as directed by the government, stopped shaving their eyebrows and making their teeth black. Both the emperor and the empress encouraged Western attire by appearing in public in Western-styled clothing and Western-styled haircuts. In the midst of the Westernization of Japan, there arose a concern to preserve Japanese values and traditions, specifically Confucian ethics and Shinto rituals, both of which became part of the Japanese educational system during the 1880s.[220] I will end this section with an brief excerpt from Fukuzawa Yukichi who promoted Westernization during Meiji Japan:

> To plan our course now, therefore, our country cannot afford to wait for the enlightenment of our neighbors and to cooperate in building Asia up. Rather, we should leave their ranks to join the camp of the civilized countries of the West. Even when dealing with China and Korea, we need not have special scruples simply because they are our neighbors, but should behave toward them as the westerners do. One who befriends an evil person cannot avoid being involved in his notoriety. In spirit, then, we break with our evil friends of Eastern Asia.[221]

---

[220] Ebrey, Walthall, and Palais, 337-352.
[221] Ebrey, Walthall, and Palais, 331.

South East Asia's Diverse Response to Western Culture

In the early twentieth century, Indonesians who were ruled by the Dutch as a colony responded to Western culture by seeking their identity in Islam. The 1912 Java-founded Islamic movement, Way of Muhammad, advocated that Indonesia become an Islamic state. In the same year, a political Islamic party was founded, the Islamic Union. By 1919, two million Indonesians were members of this party. Even though Marxism is essentially atheistic, after 1917 members of the Islamic Union began looking to Marxism as a source of inspiration. In 1920, the Marxists of the Islamic Union founded their own revolutionary party called the Indonesian Communist Party. In 1926, the Indonesia government successfully defeated a political rebellion begun by the Indonesian Communist Party, and then executed its leaders.[222]

In 1928, the Indonesian Nationalist Party, founded by Sukarno (1901-1970) rose to prominence. This party was a synthesis of Marxism, Nationalism, and Islam and one of its slogan's was "one nation-Indonesia, one people-Indonesian, one language-Indonesian."[223] The Dutch responded to the goals stated in the slogan by arresting Sukarno in 1929 and imprisoning him. His party, however, continued to attract followers. In 1942, during World War II, the Dutch rulers were replaced by Japanese occupiers. Soon after the war ended in 1945 with Japan defeated by the Allies, Sukarno declared Indonesia independent. He was then appointed as

---

[222] Craig Lockhard, *Southeast Asia in World History* (Oxford: Oxford University Press, 2009), 136-138.

[223] Lockhard, 138.

Indonesia's president.[224]

Similar to Indonesia, the British colony of Burma also sought its identity in a religion, but in Buddhism which some classify as more of a philosophy than a religion. There is even a saying that epitomizes this identification, "To be Burman is to be Buddhist." A few years after World War II ended, Burma gained its independence from Britain in 1948. About a decade later, in 1960, Buddhism became the official state religion of Burma.[225]

Vietnam was similar to Indonesia in the sense that Vietnam was eventually united by communist philosophy. We will study this more in depth when we focus on the Vietnam War (1955-1975) in chapter eleven. This war was prepared by a variety of movements ranging from transforming Vietnam according to Western culture to rejecting Western influence by seeking independence from France. One example of a violent reaction to Western rule was personified in Phan Dinh Phung, who in 1885 led a guerrilla army against the French. His revolt was unsuccessful, and he died the following year. However, he inspired others to follow suit. Phan Boi Chau continued Phan Dinh Phung's legacy by championing a violent overthrow of the French. Even though Phan Boi Chau (1867-1940) was placed under house arrest by the French, from 1925 to his death in 1940, he inspired many Vietnamese to seek freedom from French domination. In contrast to Phan Boi Chau, Phan Chau Trinh advocated a gradual and not sudden way to

---

[224] Lockhard, 136-138; Nicola Frost, *Indonesia* (Herndon: Stylus Publishing, 2002), 11.

[225] David I. Steinberg, *Burma/Myanmar, What Everyone Needs to Know* (Oxford: Oxford University Press, 2010), 32, 43.

Vietnamese independence.[226] Prior to independence, he wanted his country to learn from the West in a similar, but also different, way as the Japanese did. One way he stated this is as follows:

> I wonder why you and your friend do not open your eyes and look at the examples of East Asia. Very clever, when facing European civilization. With one slash Japan cut its old customs and began to follow the new way. The Japanese became arrogant to the Chinese, they became arrogant to the Koreans. [sic] The two countries, Japan and Korea, could not decide what to do with the old habits, refusing to follow the new way. When the Japanese achieved modernization, they scorned their fellow Asians. China and Korea began to wake up, but they were still confused about what to do at that time. With regard to ourselves, we have also been scorned, but we decided to close our eyes. We have continued in our self-destructive habits. Now we open our eyes, but still look for a dream without facing the truth and finding a way to go. What can we expect of our country? What is the nation? Shall we wait for our grandchildren, or our great-grandchildren?[227]

Vietnam did not follow the gradual path of change advocated by Phan Chau Trinh, but rather, the sudden path towards change proposed by Ho Chi Minh, who wanted to violently sever Vietnam's Western connections. Ho Chi Minh (1890-1969), whose name means He Who Enlightens,

---

[226] Lockhard, 138-141; Chu Trihn Phan, *Phan Chau Trinh and His Political Writings* (Ithaca: Southeast Asia Program Publications, 2009), 7-8.

[227] Lockhard, 138-141; Phan, 7-8.

changed his name several times before keeping Ho Chi Minh. At one point he even changed his name to Nguyen O Phap, which means He Who Hates the French.[228] He joined the French Communist Party since the party supported ending French colonies. In 1930, Ho Chi Minh founded his own communist party called the Indochinese Communist Party. The Vietnamese Communists sought to end all foreign occupation whether from their Asian neighbors, China and Japan, or from France. For this reason, Vietnamese communism was decidedly nationalistic.[229] As we will see in chapter eleven, Ho Chi Minh's communist party successfully united Vietnam under communism after defeating Western powers in the Vietnam War (1955-1975).

---

[228] Lockhard, 140.
[229] Lockhard, 139-141.

Quiz 9

1. (5 Points) Discuss Korea's response to the 1800s and 1900s to Western imperialism. Include the following in your answer: Christianity and Confucianism, the 1886 French and Korean Treaty, King Gojong, and the Kabo reform.

2. (7 Points) Discuss China's response to the 1800s and 1900s to Western imperialism. Include the following in your answer: Christianity and Hong Xiuquan, Feng Guifen and Western Technology, Empress Cixi, Sun Yatsen and his Nationalist Party.

3. (7 Points) Discuss Japan's response to the 1800s and 1900s to Western imperialism. Include the following in your answer: 1825 and the shogunate, the shogunate and U.S. gunboat diplomacy, the emperor vs. the shogunate, Meiji Japan and Westernization.

4. (5 Points) Discuss South East's Asia's response to the 1800s and 1900s to Western imperialism. Include the following in your answer: Islam, Buddhism, Marxism, Phan Chau Trinh vs. Phan Boi Chau.

Chapter 10: Modern East Asian Imperialism

Introduction

Japan distinguished itself from other Asian nations by imitating Western Imperialism to such an extent that it became an empire and dominated other Asian nations. In the First Sino-Japanese War (1894-1895), Japan defeated China and in so doing replaced China as the number one Asian power. Soon after the war, Japan also replaced China's dominance over Korea, as was touched upon in the previous chapter. Even though King Gojong attempted to make Korea independent from either China or Japan by founding the Korean empire in 1897, his achievement was short-lived. In 1910, Japan forced Emperor Gojong to abdicate, and then in 1910 annexed Korea.

Before doing so, though, Japan defeated Russia in the Russo-Japanese War (1904-1905). This was essential for Japan to do in order to gain dominance since Russia, aware of Japan's rising power, had in 1896 allied itself with China with the Li-Lobanov treaty, was given a lease by China over the Liaodong Peninsula, and had also allied itself with King Gojong's government. In order to reduce Russian influence in Asia, Japan demanded that the Russian-controlled territory in China, including Port Arthur in the Liaodong

Peninsula, be turned over to Japan. This officially took pace with the signing of the 1905 Portsmouth Treaty between Russia and Japan.[230] Japan's defeat of China, defeat of Russia, and its annexation of Korea in 1910 signaled the beginning of Japan's colonial rule. Japan's colonial rule continued into World War II and concluded in 1945 with Japan's defeat by the Allies.

Japan's Imperial Rule

Japan's imperial rule of the twentieth century can be divided into three phases: 1910-1919, 1919-1931, and 1931-1945. During these three phases of time, Japan gained direct control over both Korea and China. The 1910 Japanese annexation of Korea began the first phase. In this first phase, Japan transformed Korea into a closely controlled, monitored state called the Government-General of Chosen. Under this government, Koreans were not allowed to participate in political matters, the Korean economy was placed at the

---

[230] "Treaty of Shimonoseki Signed at Shimonoseki 17 April 1895," Taiwan Documents Project, http://www.taiwandocuments.org/shimonoseki01.htm (accessed February 1, 2015). Entered into Force 8 May 1895 by the exchange of the instruments of ratification at Chefoo http://www.taiwandocuments.org/shimonoseki01.htm; "The Treaty of Portsmouth," http://www.portsmouthpeacetreaty.com/process/peace/TreatyText.pdf (accessed February 1, 2015); H. Rogger, *Russia in the Age of Modernization and Revolution 1881-1917* (London: Routledge, 1983), 176; Djun Kil Kim, *The History of Korea*, 2nd Edition (Santa Barbara: ABC-CLIO, LLC, 2014), 123-127, 134-146; Patricia Ebrey, Anne Walthall, and James Palais, *East Asia: A Cultural, Social, and Political History* (Belmont: Wadsworth, 2009), 365-368; Jurgen Kleiner, *Korea, a Century of Change* (Boston: World Scientific, 2001), 17-22.

service of Japan, and Koreans were severely punished for even minor legal infractions. In order to prevent a military uprising, Japan dissolved the Korean army.[231]

The second phase began on March 1st, 1919, when Koreans protested their oppressive Japanese overlords with the March First Movement, also known as the Samil Movement. In this movement, thirty-three Koreans signed a declaration of independence from Japan and then peacefully staged a march. They were inspired by the U.S. president Woodrow Wilson's 14 Points that he first presented on January 8, 1918, to the U.S. Congress and also presented at the Paris Peace Conference of 1919 that set the terms for the defeated Central Powers of World War I. According to point number five there is to be:

> A free, open-minded, and absolutely impartial adjustment of all colonial claims, based upon a strict observance of the principle that in determining all such questions of sovereignty the interests of the populations concerned must have equal weight with the equitable claims of the government whose title is to be determined.[232]

In other words, nations, such as Korea, are to be allowed to be freed from colonial powers in order to self-determine and govern themselves. The U.S. State Department responded to the self-determination movement by directing its ambassador to Japan to reassure Japan that the U.S. will not

---

[231] Ebrey, Walthall, and Palais, 391; Ki-baik Lee, *A New History of Korea* (Cambridge: Harvard University Press, 1984), 312.

[232] "President Woodrow Wilson's Fourteen Points," 8 January, 1918, Avalon Project, http://avalon.law.yale.edu/20th_century/wilson14.asp, (accessed February 21, 2016).

support a Korean independence movement. Despite the lack of support from the U.S., the March First Movement still publicly supported Korean independence from Japan. It began with 33 Korean leaders reading a Declaration of Independence in a restaurant of Seoul. Afterwards, they peacefully surrendered themselves to the police. This was followed by similar demonstrations throughout Korea. Japanese officials responded with violence. Approximately 7,000 Koreans were killed by Japanese-controlled police and soldiers, 46,000 Koreans were arrested, thousands were tortured, and the leaders of the movement were hunted down. Later, though, in order to decrease motivation for more revolts, Japan allowed Koreans a limited amount of free speech, assembly, and business practice.[233]

~ Korean Independence Proclamation of 1919 ~

We herewith proclaim the independence of Korea and the liberty of the Korean people. We tell it to the world in witness of the equality of all nations, and we pass it on to our posterity as their inherent right.

We make this proclamation, having back of us a history of forty-three centuries and 20,000,000 united, loyal people. We take this step to insure to our children for all time to come, life and liberty in accord with the awakening conscience of this new era. This is the clear leading of God, the moving principle of the present age, the just claim of the whole human race. It is something

---

[233] Ebrey, Walthall, and Palais, 391-397; Jitendra Uttam, *The Political Economy of Korea: Transition, Transformation and Turnaround* (New York: Palgrave Macmillan, 2014), 81-82; Theodore McNelly, *Sources in Modern East Asian History and Politics* (New York: Meredith Corporation, 1967), 90.

that cannot be stamped out, or stifled, or gagged, or suppressed by any means.

Victims of an older age, when brute force and the spirit of plunder ruled, we have come after these long thousands of years to experience the agony of ten years of foreign oppression, with every loss of the right to live, every restriction of the freedom of thought, every damage done to the dignity of life, every opportunity lost for a share in the intelligent advance of the age in which we live. ...[234]

In 1931, Japan extended its imperial rule by invading the large Northeast Chinese region of Manchuria, overthrowing the governor and establishing a state controlled by the Japanese. During this phase, Japan re-established its strict police state in Korea. Japan did so to build up its military. As a result, Koreans were forced into labor, were conscripted in the military, were required to learn Japanese, were required to worship the Japanese emperor, and even had to call themselves by Japanese names. Thousands of Korean and Chinese women during this third phase of brutal oppression were also forced by the Japanese to meet the Japanese troops' sexual desires. They were euphemistically called "comfort women."[235] One reason why the Japanese military instituted sexual slavery was, as reported by the Japanese Ministry of War Medical Bureau by the chief of the Medical Section in the 21st Army, Matsumura Takeshi:

To prevent the spread of sexually transmitted diseases, we have been importing one comfort woman for every 100 soldiers. That amounts to 1,400 to 1,600 people so

---

[234] McNelly, 90.
[235] Ebrey, Walthall, and Palais, 391-392, 397.

far. Treatment is being given at Hakuai Hospital with comfort station operators bearing the costs. Tests for syphilis are conducted twice a week.[236]

The Japanese Empire During World War II

World War II is commonly understood as beginning on September 1st, 1939, when Germany invaded Poland and France reacted by declaring war with Germany. This war was preceded by Japan's aggressive imperialism in the East. Before Germans invaded Poland, Japan had been waging a war with China called the Second Sino-Japanese War (1937-1941). The year before the Second Sino-Japanese War, Japan strengthened its alliance with Nazi Germany by signing an anti-communist pact by which they opposed the Soviet Union. In 1937, Fascist Italy joined the pact. The excerpt below is from the 1937 version of the pact:

> The Italian Government, the Government of the German Reich, and the Imperial Government of Japan,
>
> Considering that the Communist International continues constantly to imperil the civilized world in the Occident and Orient, disturbing and destroying peace and order,
>
> Considering that only close collaboration looking to the maintenance of peace and order can limit and remove that peril,
>
> Considering that Italy - who with the advent of the Fascist

---

[236] Yoskiaki Yoshimi, *Comfort Women: Sexual Slavery in the Japanese Military During World War II*, trans. Suzanne O'Brien (New York: Columbia University Press, 2000), 56.

regime has with inflexible determination combated that peril and rid her territory of the Communist International - has decided to align herself against the common enemy along with Germany and Japan, who for their part are animated by like determination to defend themselves against the Communist International.[237]

During World War II, Japan continued its alliance with Nazi Germany and with Fascist Italy. In an attempt to take out the U.S. threat with a pre-emptive strike, on December 7, 1941, Japan bombed Hawaii's Pearl Harbor. The next day, December 8th, the U.S. Congress approved the U.S. to fight on the side of the Allies. For about three years, the U.S. fought in World War II. The War ended when on May 8th of 1945 Germany officially surrendered and on August 15th of the same year Japan surrendered.[238] The map below shows Japan in 1942 when it was at the height of its imperial power.

---

[237] "Protocol Concluded by Italy, Germany, and Japan, at Rome, November 6, 1937," Avalon Project, http://avalon.law.yale.edu/wwii/tri3.asp, (accessed February 21, 2016).

[238] Antony Beevor, *The Second World War* (New York: Bay Back Books, 2012), 1, 22, 23, 256, 269; "Anti-Comintern Pact, German-Japanese Agreement and Supplementary Protocol, Signed at Berlin, November 25, 1936," Yale Law School, Lillian Goldman Law Library, The Avalon Project, http://avalon.law.yale.edu/wwii/tri1.asp (accessed February 12, 2015).

Fr. Peter Samuel Kucer, MSA

~ The Empire of Japan in 1942 ~

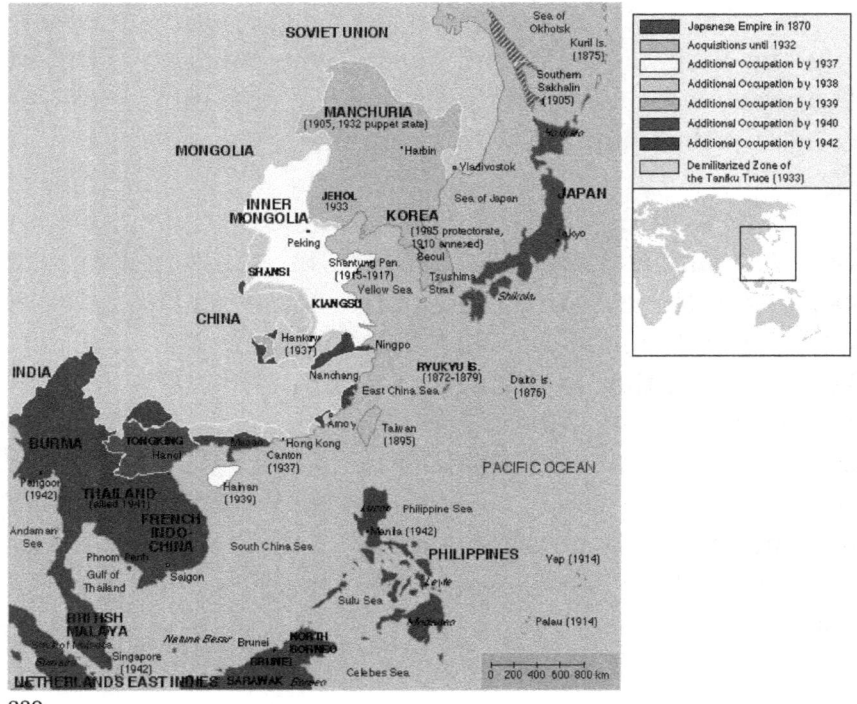

239

The Japanese Empire Ends

Japan surrendered after the U.S. dropped nuclear weapons on Hiroshima and Nagasaki. On August 6th 1945, the U.S. dropped the atomic bomb "Little Boy" over Hiroshima. Upon detonating the bomb instantly killed approximately 70,000 people. In exploding, people and buildings were instantly vaporized. Emperor Hirohito, though, only surren-

---

239 Author unidentified, "Maximum extent of the Japanese Empire," map, https://commons.wikimedia.org/wiki/File:Japanese_Empire2.png (accessed February 20, 2016). See link for color.

dered after a second U.S. atomic bomb, "Fat man," was dropped over Nagasaki on August 9th, 1945.[240]

~ Before and After the Bombing of Nagasaki ~

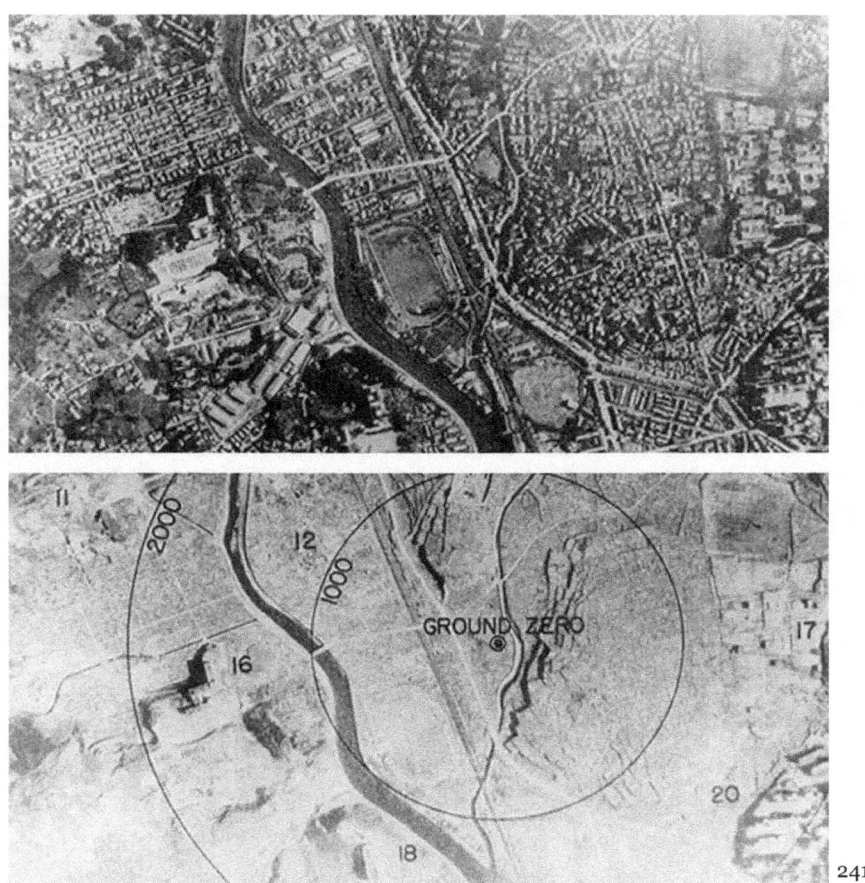
[241]

One of the most prominent bishops of the time,

---

[240] Jamie Poolos, *The Atomic Bombings of Hiroshima and Nagasaki* (New York: Chelsea House, 2008), 95-103.
[241] Fastfission, "Nagasaki, Japan, before and after the atomic bombing of August 9, 1945," photographs, https://commons.wikimedia.org/wiki/File%3ANagasaki_1945_-_Before_and_after_(adjusted).jpg, (accessed February 20, 2016).

Archbishop Fulton Sheen in commenting on the U.S. decision to drop an atomic bomb over Hiroshima, described this nuclear explosion over a civilian population as changing the world psychologically since it:

> blotted out boundaries. There was no longer a boundary between the military and the civilian, between the helper and the helped, between the wounded and the nurse and the doctor, and the living and the dead. For even the living who escaped the bomb were already half dead. So we broke down boundaries and limits and from that time on the world has said we want no one limiting me. ... You want no restraint, no boundaries. I have to do what I want to do.[242]

Years later, on the fortieth anniversary of Hiroshima's atomic bombing by the U.S. in a radio message to the people of Japan, Pope St. John Paul II strongly condemned the use of nuclear bombs:

> To speak of Hiroshima and of Nagasaki is to become vividly aware of the immense pain and horror and death that human beings are capable of inflicting upon one another. But it is also to be conscious of the fact that such a tragic destiny is not inevitable. It can and must be avoided. Our world needs to regain confidence in its capacity to choose moral good over evil.

---

[242] "The Anniversary of Hiroshima: John Paul II and Fulton Sheen on the Bomb and Conversion," August 6, 2014, Catholic World Report, http://www.catholicworldreport.com/Item/3293/the_anniversary_of_hiroshima_john_paul_ii_and_fulton_sheen_on_the_bomb_and_conversion.aspx (accessed February 21, 2016). See https://www.youtube.com/watch?v=coM_ZIc-N4M.

The Catholic Church is irrevocably committed to the challenge of promoting genuine peace between peoples and nations, against war and death. The Church sees this challenge as a duty before God, the Lord of Life, and as inexorable service of love towards every man, woman and child on this earth.

I wish to take this opportunity to repeat something which I believe requires much thought. The vast majority of people want peace. ... It is my deep conviction . . . and is, I hope, the intuition of many men and women of good will, that war has its origins in the human heart. It is man who kills and not his sword, or in our day, his missiles ...

It is therefore the human "heart" that must change: from a new heart, peace is born. In this perspective Hiroshima, from August 6, 1945, and Nagasaki from three days later, have a unique responsibility before the world. The people of these two cities can proclaim, with the force of their own experience, the value of life over death, of peace over war.

Hiroshima is a living witness to what can happen but need not and should never happen. When I visited Hiroshima in 1981 I wished to emphasize that "one must affirm and reaffirm, again and again, that the waging of war is not inevitable or unchangeable". ...[243]

---

[243] John Paul II, "Radio Message of Pope John Paul II to the People of Japan," Tuesday, 6 August 1985, w2.vatican.va., http://w2.vatican.va/content/john-paul-ii/en/speeches/1985/august/documents/hf_jp-ii_spe_19850806_radiomessaggio-giappone.html (accessed February 21, 2016).

Quiz 10

1. (Eight Points) Describe how Japan imitated Western Imperialism. Include the following in your answer: First Sino-Japanese War, Russo-Japanese War, the three phases of Japan's Imperial rule. When referring to the three phases include a few specifics for each one.

2. (Four Points) Explain why and how Koreans in 1919 first began protesting Japanese rule. Include the following in your response: Woodrow Wilson's 14 Points, March First Movement, U.S. response, and Japanese response.

3. (Four Points) With respect to Bishop Fulton Sheen and John Paul II's excerpts in Chapter 10, discuss the moral implications and effects of the atomic bombings of Hiroshima and Nagasaki.

Chapter 11: East Asia Post World War II

Introduction

World War II ended Japan's Empire and left Japan in a devastated, uncertain state. After the war, 6.6 million Japanese found themselves without protection in lands of the Allies. Around 570,000 of these Japanese, in particular men, were sent by the Soviets to Siberian labor camps. Many of the stranded Japanese women and children suffered an even worse fate by being killed and/or raped by Soviet soldiers. The Chinese also turned on their former overlords by killing Japanese present in Manchuria.

Those Japanese who were able to safely return to their homeland encountered a country in the midst of an economic depression, few jobs, the harsh winter of 1945-1946, numerous widows, orphans, and the maimed and crippled of the war. During this time, the U.S. through General Douglas MacArthur governed Japan from 1945 to 1952. When the U.S. handed back political power to Japan in 1952, Japan not only successfully gained control over its political life and economy but became one of the world's strongest free market economies with a growth rate from 1954 to 1971 that was number two in the world, behind the

United States.[244]

Following our study on Post-World War II Japan, we will turn our attention to another East Asia territory, Korea, and to one South East Asian country, Vietnam. Both Korea and Vietnam were devastated by a major war.

Post-World War II Japan

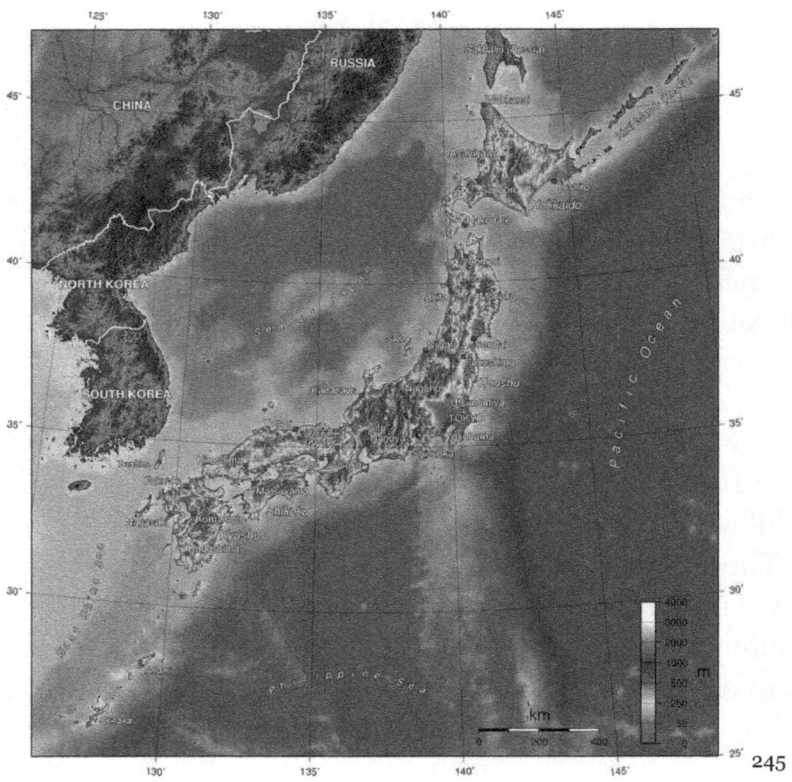

[245]

---

[244] Patricia Ebrey, Anne Walthall, and James Palais, *East Asia: A Cultural, Social, and Political History* (Belmont: Wadsworth, 2009), 445, 453.

[245] Electionworld, "Topographic map of the Japanese archipelago," map, https://commons.wikimedia.org/wiki/File:Japan_topo_en.jpg (accessed February 29, 2016).

We will begin this section with the internment of Japanese Americans by the U.S. during World War II. Shortly after the bombing of Pearl Harbor on December 7th, 1941, President Franklin D. Roosevelt with his Executive Order 9066 authorized the Secretary of War and Military Commanders to designate military areas in the U.S. in order to protect "against espionage and against sabotage."[246] As a result of the Executive Order, all people in the U.S. who were determined by the Secretary of War and Military Commanders as a threat to U.S. national security were relocated from the western coast of the U.S. to internment camps deeper within the U.S. Within the span of six months about 122,000 men, women and children of Japanese descent who were living on the U.S. West Coast were relocated to ten fenced in guarded camps. The ten camps, which were essentially prisons, were located in Wyoming, California, Utah, Arizona, Colorado, and Idaho.[247]

---

[246] "Executive Order 9066: Resulting in the Relocation of Japanese (1942)," our documents.gov., http://www.ourdocuments.gov/doc.php?flash=true&doc=74 (accessed February 23, 2016).

[247] "Executive Order 9066."

Fr. Peter Samuel Kucer, MSA

248

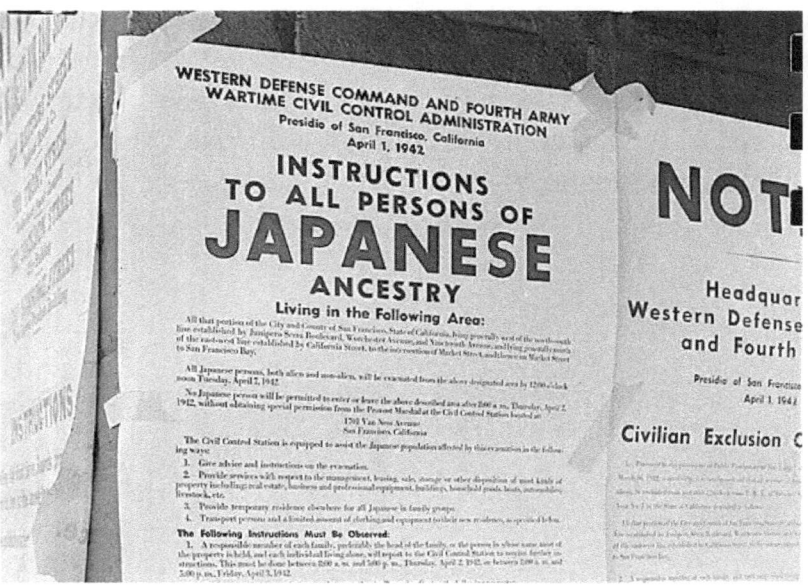

249

---

²⁴⁸ Author unidentified, "Newspaper headlines of Japanese Relocation," photograph, https://commons.wikimedia.org/wiki/File%3ANewspaper_headlines_of_Japanese_Relocation_-_NARA_-_195535.jpg (accessed February 23, 2016).

²⁴⁹ Department of the Interior. War Relocation Authority, "Exclusion Order posted to direct Japanese Americans living in

Below is an eyewitness account of the brutal treatment of Japanese in a Post-World War II Soviet, Siberian work camp.

~ Kagawa Haruyoshi's Account of a Siberian Work Camp ~

Our internment camp was built on Siberian tundra. It was said that the internees there numbered a thousand or fifteen hundred men. They say that over one winter five hundred men died of illness or starvation...Meals were gruel served in the lids of the men's mess tins. With only this to eat the men worked on building the roadbed for the railroad or on logging operations. The old Japanese military system was kept as it was, with its generous treatment of higher-ranking officers and poor treatment of lower-ranking, younger soldiers. This meant that the younger soldiers were the first to die.

The dead bodies were piled up in the empty barracks in the camp. When the men died, they were stripped of their clothes, and their bodies froze stiff as logs. Graves couldn't be dug fast enough to keep up with the deaths because the earth in Siberia was frozen. Large bonfires were lit on the frozen tundra to melt the surface. With steel pikes, the earth was dug one and two millimeters at a time. After a certain depth was reached, a number of bodies were thrown into the pit together. Because they were frozen, the bones broke and shattered. This went on day and night. I will never forget the bonfires lighting up

---

the first San Francisco section to evacuate," photograph, https://commons.wikimedia.org/wiki/File%3APosted_Japanese_American_Exclusion_Order.jpg, (accessed February 23, 2016).

the night sky for as long as I live.[250]

From the beginning of the post-World War II Japanese persecution until 1952, the U.S. occupied Japan through the rule of General Douglas MacArthur. During this time, Japan underwent political and economic reforms and was demilitarized. One of the first significant political reforms occurred on January 1, 1946, when the Japanese emperor formally announced he was not divine but only human. This is currently referred to as the "Declaration of Humanity." In it, the emperor asserted:

> The ties between Us and Our people have always stood upon mutual trust and affection. They do not depend upon mere legends and myths. They are not predicated on the false conception that the Emperor is divine, and that the Japanese people are superior to other races and fated to rule the world.[251]

Near the end of 1946, the emperor promulgated on November 3rd a new constitution. See below for excepts from this constitution. Notice that the emperor promulgated the 1946 constitution. This occurred despite Britain's desire to try the emperor as a war criminal. General MacArthur wanted to keep the emperor in his role in order to keep the country politically stable and in so doing reduce the danger of communism from gaining power in Japan.[252]

---

[250] Frank Gibney, *Senso: The Japanese Remember the Pacific War*, expanded edition, trans. Beth Cary (New York: Routledge, 2015) 222-223.

[251] "Imperial Rescript," chukai.ne.jp, http://www.chukai.ne.jp/~masago/ningen.html, (accessed February 24, 2016)

[252] Ebrey, Walthall, and Palais, 448.

~ The Constitution of Japan, 1946 ~

...
CHAPTER I. THE EMPEROR

Article 1. The Emperor shall be the symbol of the State and of the unity of the people, deriving his position from the will of the people with whom resides sovereign power.

Article 2. The Imperial Throne shall be dynastic and succeeded to in accordance with the Imperial House law passed by the Diet.

Article 3. The advice and approval of the Cabinet shall be required for all acts of the Emperor in matters of state, and the Cabinet shall be responsible therefor.

Article 4. The Emperor shall perform only such acts in matters of state as are provided for in this Constitution and he shall not have powers related to government

(2) The Emperor may delegate the performance of his acts in matters of state as may be provided by law.

...

Article 6. The Emperor shall appoint the Prime Minister as designated by the Diet.

...

CHAPTER II. RENUNCIATION OF WAR

Article 9. Aspiring sincerely to an international peace based on justice and order, the Japanese people forever renounce war as a sovereign right of the nation and the threat or use of force as a mean of settling international disputes.

(2) In order to accomplish the aim of the preceding paragraph, land, sea, and air forces, as well as other war potential, will never be maintained. The right of belligerency of the state will not be recognized.

CHAPTER III. RIGHTS AND DUTIES OF THE PEOPLE

Article 10. The conditions necessary for being a Japanese national shall be determined by law.

Article 11. The people shall not be prevented from enjoying any of the fundamental human rights. These fundamental human rights guaranteed to the people by this Constitution shall be conferred upon the people of this and future generations as eternal and inviolate rights.
...
Article 13. All of the people shall be respected as individuals. Their right to life, liberty, and the pursuit of happiness shall, to the extent that it does not interfere with the public welfare, be the supreme consideration in legislation and in other governmental affairs.

Article 14. All of the people are equal under the law and there shall be no discrimination in political, economic or social relations because of race, creed, sex, social status or family origin.

...

Article 15. The people have the inalienable right to choose their public officials and to dismiss them.

...

Article 19. Freedom of thought and conscience shall not be violated.

Article 20. Freedom of religion is guaranteed to all. No religious organization shall receive any privileges from the State nor exercise any political authority.

...

Article 21. Freedom of assembly and association as well as speech, press and all other forms of expression are guaranteed.

...

Article 23. Academic freedom is guaranteed.

...

CHAPTER IV. THE DIET

Article 41. The Diet shall be the highest organ of state power, and shall be the sole law-making organ of the State.

Article 42. The Diet shall consist of two Houses, namely the House of Representatives and the House of Councilors.

Article 43. Both Houses shall consist of elected members, representative of all the people.

...

CHAPTER V. THE CABINET

Article 65. Executive power shall be vested in the Cabinet.

Article 66. The Cabinet shall consist of the Prime Minister, who shall be its head, and other Ministers of State, as provided for by law.

(2) The Prime Minister and other Minister of State must be civilians.

(3) The Cabinet, in the exercise of executive power, shall be collectively responsible to the Diet.
...

CHAPTER VI. JUDICIARY

Article 76. The whole judicial power is vested in a Supreme Court and in such inferior courts as are established by law. ...[253]

In 1952, the U.S. occupation of Japan ended. The constitution of 1946, though, continued to be the governing document for Japan and still is today. Under this constitution, Japan underwent remarkable economic growth. Factors that contributed to this economic success were both external and internal to Japan. The terms detailing Japanese surrender in 1945, called the Potsdam Declaration, allowed Japan to have continued access, but not control of, raw material it had taken from its former colonies under the

---

[253] "The Constitution of Japan, 1946," Gutenberg.org, http://www.gutenberg.org/cache/epub/612/pg612-images.html, (accessed February 25, 2016).

condition that the industries Japan uses these material in will not "enable her to re-arm for war."[254] Internally, as a consequence of the Japanese value of education, Japan was blessed with an educated work force that developed prior to and during World War II. The mentioned internal and external factors enabled Japan to become in the 1950s the world's greatest shipbuilder and a successful exporter of a variety of goods.[255]

The Korean War

World War II was followed by two other major wars: the Korean War (1950-1953) and the Vietnam War (1955-1975). The Vietnam War sparked and coincided with Cambodia's civil war (1967-1975). We will begin with the Korean War. On August 8th of 1945, two days after the U.S. dropped an atomic bomb on Hiroshima and a day before the U.S. dropped an atomic bomb over Nagasaki, the Soviet Union declared war on Japan. Then on August 10th, a day after Japan surrendered, the Soviet Union moved troops to northern Korea in order to establish a pro-Soviet Korean government. The Soviet expansion disturbed President Truman and his administration who had hoped that with Japan defeated, all of Korea would fall under U.S. influence. Since this did not seem likely, the U.S. proposed to Stalin that Korea be divided roughly in half by the 38th parallel north. Stalin agreed to the

---

[254] "Potsdam Declaration," Birth of the Constitution of Japan, http://www.ndl.go.jp/constitution/e/etc/c06.html (accessed February 25, 2016); Patricia Ebrey, Anne Walthall, and James Palais, *East Asia: A Cultural, Social, and Political History* (Belmont: Wadsworth, 2009), 452.

[255] Ebrey, Walthall, and Palais, 453.

proposal on August 15th.[256]

About five years later, on June 25th, 1950, the North Korean army, backed by the Soviet Union and China, invaded South Korea. Even so, this did not amount to, explained the U.S. Secretary of State Dean Acheson, "a *causus belli* [cause of war] against the Soviet Union."[257] However, Acheson goes on to write, "Equally plainly, it was an open, undisguised challenge to our internationally accepted position as the protector of South Korea, an area of great importance to the security of American-occupied Japan."[258] The U.S. and South Korean troops, with the support of the United Nations, fought back. On July 27th, 1953, the war ended basically where it began. Northern Korea remained controlled by a communist, Soviet-backed government. South Korea, on the other hand, looked to the U.S. for guidance and developed into a capitalistic-democratic nation.[259] The war casualties were about one-and-a-half million, 142,000 for the UN, mainly U.S. troops, and about a million Koreans.[260] The July 27th, 1953, Korean War Armistice Agreement that brought an end to the war stated in its preamble:

> The undersigned, the Commander-in-Chief, United Nations Command, on the one hand, and the Supreme Commander of the Korean People's Army and the Com-

---

[256] Steven Hugh Lee, *The Korean War* (New York: Routledge, 2001), 21.

[257] Lee, 133.

[258] From Dean Acheson's 1969 explanation in *Present at the Creation: May Years in the State Department*. Steven Hugh Lee, *The Korean War* (New York: Routledge, 2001), 133.

[259] Max Hastings, *The Korean War* (New York: Simon & Schuster Inc., 1987), 11, 15, 25, 27, 45-54, 230-234.

[260] Hastings, 9.

mander of the Chinese People's Volunteers, on the other hand, in the interest of stopping the Korean conflict, with its great toll of suffering and bloodshed on both sides, and with the objective of establishing an armistice which will insure a complete cessation of hostilities and of all acts of armed force in Korea until a final peaceful settlement is achieved, do individually, collectively, and mutually agree to accept and to be bound and governed by the conditions and terms of armistice set forth in the following Articles and Paragraphs, which said conditions and terms are intended to be purely military in character to pertain solely to the belligerents in Korea.[261]

The peace settlement referred to in the preamble did not occur for another six and a half decades when on April 27, 2018, South Korean President Moon Jae-in and North Korean leader Kim Jong-un signed the Panmunjom Declaration for Peace, Prosperity and Unification on the Korean Peninsula committing the two countries to talks intended to formally end the conflict.[262] In other words, a peace treaty between North Korea and South Korea was not signed at the time. Effectively, this meant that the conflict did not end but rather turned into a cold war marked by occasional hot flare ups.[263]

---

[261] "Korean War Armistice Agreement, July 27, 1953," archives.gov., http://www.archives.gov/global-pages/larger-image.html?i=/historical-docs/doc-content/images/korean-war-armistice-l.jpg, (accessed February 27, 2016).

[262] James Griffiths, "North and South Korea Vow to End the Korean War in Historic Accord," CNN, April 27, 2018, https://www.cnn.com/2018/04/27/asia/korean-summit-intl/index.html (accessed October 21, 2019)

[263] FoxNews.com, "North Korea says it's in 'state of war' with South Korea," foxnews.com, http://www.foxnews.com/politics/2013/03/30/north-korea-says-it-in-state-war-with-south-korea.html, (accessed February 27, 2016).

Fr. Peter Samuel Kucer, MSA

The Vietnam War and Cambodia

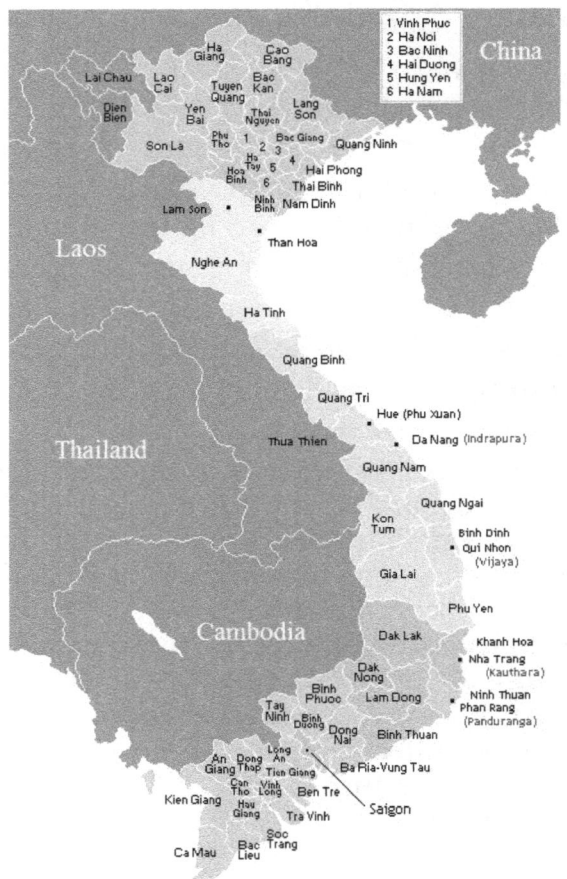

264

The Vietnam War (1955-1975) was another proxy war

---

²⁶⁴ By English: Created by CGlassey and uploaded by Electionworld [GFDL (http://www.gnu.org/copyleft/fdl.html), CC-BY-SA-3.0 (http://creativecommons.org/licenses/by-sa/3.0/) or CC BY 2.5 (http://creativecommons.org/licenses/by/2.5)], via Wikimedia Commons, "Map of Vietnam showing the conquest of the south (the *Nam tiến*), 1069–1757 900 1100 1475 1650 1760," map, https://commons.wikimedia.org/wiki/File%3AVietnam_Expand1.gif (accessed February 29, 2016).

between the U.S. and the Soviets as well as being a civil war of Vietnam. As a proxy war, the Soviet Union and communist China, through the North Vietnamese, fought the U.S.-backed South Vietnam military. The U.S. fought in this war for the same reason it fought in the Korean War. This reason is explained in the Truman Doctrine that was instituted as reaction to the Greek civil war (1946-1949) between communists and anticommunists and to other similar events. In his March 12, 1947, address before congress, President Harry S. Truman described this doctrine by stating:

...

> One of the primary objectives of the foreign policy of the United States is the creation of conditions in which we and other nations will be able to work out a way of life free from coercion. This was a fundamental issue in the war with Germany and Japan. Our victory was won over countries which sought to impose their will, and their way of life, upon other nations.
>
> To ensure the peaceful development of nations, free from coercion, the United States has taken a leading part in establishing the United Nations. The United Nations is designed to make possible lasting freedom and independence for all its members. We shall not realize our objectives, however, unless we are willing to help free peoples to maintain their free institutions and their national integrity against aggressive movements that seek to impose upon them totalitarian regimes. This is no more than a frank recognition that totalitarian regimes imposed on free peoples, by direct or indirect aggression, undermine the foundations of international peace and hence the security of the United States.

The peoples of a number of countries of the world have recently had totalitarian regimes forced upon them against their will. The Government of the United States has made frequent protests against coercion and intimidation, in violation of the Yalta agreement, in Poland, Rumania, and Bulgaria. I must also state that in a number of other countries there have been similar developments.

At the present moment in world history nearly every nation must choose between alternative ways of life. The choice is too often not a free one.

One way of life is based upon the will of the majority, and is distinguished by free institutions, representative government, free elections, guarantees of individual liberty, freedom of speech and religion, and freedom from political oppression.

The second way of life is based upon the will of a minority forcibly imposed upon the majority. It relies upon terror and oppression, a controlled press and radio; fixed elections, and the suppression of personal freedoms.

I believe that it must be the policy of the United States to support free peoples who are resisting attempted subjugation by armed minorities or by outside pressures.

I believe that we must assist free peoples to work out their own destinies in their own way....[265]

---

[265] President Harry S. Truman, "Truman Doctrine: President Harry S. Truman's Address Before a Joint Session of Congress,

In accordance with the Truman Doctrine, the U.S aided South Vietnam in order to prevent a totalitarian, communist regime in gaining control over Vietnam.[266] Despite South Vietnam's military defense of their land as aided by the U.S., in 1975, North Vietnam successfully defeated South Vietnam and then united Vietnam as one country under a communist government.[267]

During a good part of the Vietnam War, a civil war also erupted in Cambodia (1967-1975). The two sides of the Cambodian Civil War was the Community Khmer Rouge party, supported by North Vietnam, and the Kingdom of Cambodia, supported by the U.S. and South Vietnam. The civil war was followed by a "systematic political slaughter"[268] led by Pol Pot's party that was responsible for the deaths of one to three million people, of which around 200,000 were executed with the rest dying from starvation, overwork, disease, and torture. The genocide ended when the Vietnamese Communist government invaded Cambodia and

---

March 12, 1947," avalon.law.yale.edu., http://avalon.law.yale.edu/20th_century/trudoc.asp (accessed February 27, 2016).

[266] The US Marshall Plan (1948-1952) is also traceable to this time. This plan was named after the Secretary of State George Marshall. Its goal was to rebuild European countries economic infrastructure, devastated by World War II, after the efficient US business model. The US provided the funds to do so as long as certain criteria were met.

[267] Mark Atwood Lawrence, *The Vietnam War: A Concise International History* (Oxford: Oxford University Press, 2008), 1-8, 36-37, 94-95.

[268] This term is used since and Dutton points out the decision to kill people at this time was not based mainly or solely race or ethnicity. Donald G. Dutton, *The Psychology of Genocide, Massacres, and Extreme Violence: Why :Normal Come to Commit Atrocities* (Westport: Praeger Security International, 2007), 31.

successfully ended this atrocity.[269]

A brief overview of Cambodia's recent history will help to understand why the genocide occurred. From 1863 to 1953, Cambodia was a protectorate of France through the French colony of French Indochina. Its protectorate status was interrupted for a few years during World War II when from 1941 to 1945 the Japanese occupied Cambodia. In 1953, Cambodia gained its independence and became ruled by Norodom Sihanouk. Even though Sihanouk was interested in a constitutional monarchy, he chose instead to rule as a strong authoritarian King. His reign lasted until 1970, the year when he was ousted from power.[270]

During the Vietnam War, Cambodia engaged in a civil war (1970-1975) between communists, led by Pol Pot, and the Constitutional Monarchy. Pol Pot was aided by China, the Soviets, and Czechoslovakia. The war ended with Pol Pot and his Communist Party the Khmer Rouge as the victors. In 1976, Pol Pot began instituting a totalitarian regime in which people in the country were forced into farming labor camps. In explaining why he did this, he asserted:

> We take agriculture as the basic factor and use the fruits of agriculture to systematically build industry in order to advance toward rapidly transforming a Cambodia marked by a backward agriculture into a Cambodia marked by a modernized agriculture. We also intend to rapidly transform the backward agricultural Cambodia into an industrialized Cambodia. [This resulted in] a national society characterized by equality, justice,

---

[269] Sean Bergin, *The Khmer Rouge and the Cambodian Genocide* (New York: The Rosen Publishing Group, 2009), 9, 36-39, 53.

[270] John Tully, *A Short History of Cambodia: From Empire to Survival* (Crows Nest: Allen & Unwin, 2005), 80, 119-121, 128.

genuine democracy and the absence of the rich, poor, exploiting and exploited classes and in an independent, united, peaceful, neutral, nonaligned and sovereign Cambodia with full territorial integrity.[271]

In order to do so his party systematically killed those they believed could make this political goal less likely to achieve. Those killed, in accordance with the slogan, "Keeping [urban dwellers] is no benefit, losing them is no loss,"[272] were people who criticized the party, foreigners, people who had an education above grade 7, people who wore glasses, and even people found guilty of publicly recalling their memories.[273] Pol Pot also saw the youth as an important means by which to institute his perfect society since they knew very little and could, he believed, be quickly made to believe in his vision.[274]

In 1978, Vietnam invaded Cambodia and ended the mass killings and brought an end of illegal border crossings from Cambodia into Vietnam. The illegal border crossings that especially infuriated the Vietnamese were done by Khmer

---

[271] Lorna Fitzsimmons, Youngsuk Chai, Bella Adams, *Asian American Literature and the Environment* (New York: Routledge, 2015), 97.

[272] David P. Chandler, *The Tragedy of Cambodian History: Politics, War, and Revolution Since 1945* (New Haven: Yale University Press, 1991), 249, 280; 31

[273] Donald G. Dutton, *The Psychology of Genocide, Massacres, and Extreme Violence: Why Normal Come to Commit Atrocities* (Westport: Praeger Security International, 2007), 31-33; Nicholas John Cull, David Holbrook Culbert, David Welch, *Propaganda and Mass Persuasion: A Historical Encyclopedia, 1500 to the Present* (Santa Barbara: ABC-CLIO, 2003), 372.

[274] Nicholas John Cull, David Holbrook Culbert, David Welch, *Propaganda and Mass Persuasion: A Historical Encyclopedia, 1500 to the Present* (Santa Barbara: ABC-CLIO, 2003), 372.

Rouge guerillas who violently raided Vietnamese villages, and in so doing displaced around half a million Vietnamese. In 1993, the UN helped to monitor elections and to establish a multiparty democracy. In the process, King Norodom Sihanouk was reinstated as King of Cambodia of a constitutional monarchy.[275]

Quiz 11

1. (Three Points) Describe in at least three ways how Japanese living outside of their country were persecuted during World War II and after World War II. Include in your answer the following: U.S. internment camps, Siberia, and Manchuria.

2. (Six Points) Describe key, specific points of the 1946 Constitution of Japan while including the following: Declaration of Humanity, the role of the emperor, war, equality, freedom, checks and balances of power.

---

[275] Tully, 192-193.

3. (Four Points) Compare and contrast the Korean war with the Vietnamese War in at least four different ways.

4. (Five Points) First, state the goal of Pol Pot for Cambodia. Then, describe at least four means which Pol Pot used to achieve this goal.

Chapter 12: Modern East Asia

Introduction

We will conclude this textbook with a look at Modern East Asia. We will begin with the so-called Asian Tigers, which have experienced remarkable economic growth. Then, we will contrast modern day China and its market socialism with its not so distant totalitarian times under Mao Ze Dong. Finally, we will look at two countries, Vietnam which is more closely aligned with the China of modern times and North Korea that closely resembles, with differences, the totalitarian model of China under Mao Ze Dong.

Asian Tigers

The Asian Tigers refer to three nations and one region which have experienced a high degree of economic growth: South Korea, Singapore, Taiwan, and Hong Kong. In describing this phenomenon that was not only evident in the Asian Tigers but also in a lesser degree in other Asian countries Michael Sarel, writing for the International Monetary Fund, states:

> Since 1960 Asia, the largest and most populous of the continents, has become richer faster than any other region of the world. Of course, this growth has not

occurred at the same pace all over the continent. The western part of Asia grew during this period at about the same rate as the rest of the world, but, as a whole, the eastern half (ten countries: China, Hong Kong, Indonesia, Japan, Korea, Malaysia, the Philippines, Singapore, Taiwan Province of China, and Thailand) turned in a superior performance, although variations in achievement can be observed here too. The worst performer was the Philippines, which grew at about 2 percent a year (in per capita terms), about equal to the average of non-Asian countries. China, Indonesia, Japan, Malaysia, and Thailand did better, achieving growth rates of 3-5 percent. This impressive achievement is, however, still modest compared with the phenomenal growth of Hong Kong, Korea, Singapore, and Taiwan Province of China, known as the "Four Tigers" because of their powerful and intimidating economic performance. The Tigers have had annual growth rates of output per person well in excess of 6 percent. These growth rates, sustained over a 30-year period, are simply amazing. While the average resident of a non-Asian country in 1990 was 72 percent richer than his parents were in 1960, the corresponding figure for the average Korean is no less than 638 percent.[276]

A surprising aspect of this astonishing growth is that, continues Sarel, "Everyone agrees that the economies of East Asia, and particularly the Four Tigers, have grown spectacularly over the past generation, but nobody seems to agree on

---

[276] Michael Sarel, "Growth in East Asia: What We Can and What We Cannot Infer," September 1996, imf.org, http://www.imf.org/external/pubs/ft/issues1/, (accessed March 1, 2016).

why."[277] It is, though, agreed that three basic economic facts contributed to the economic growth: more efficient technology, labor or manpower, and growth in durable capital goods in particular machines, buildings, and transportation. The debate centers around which one of these factors was central. Did the Asian use of more efficient technology drive the growth of capital goods and an increased work force or did the mobilization of labor and building of durable capital goods largely explain the growth? Sarel, relying on economic data, argues in part for the former position. However, he also indicates that other factors need to also be considered, especially the role of the Asian governments.

> Some argue that for Asian countries to continue to experience growth they need to allow greater economic competition, free up markets, and reduce governmental interference in markets. This position is rejected by both those who argue that in order to protect their countries from the swings of the market Asian governments need to selectively intervene. Still others reject both the free market view and the limited governmental intervention approach by simply stating it is not possible to know if a free market or a governmental protectionist approach is better for sustained economic growth. After all, it is not possible to revisit the past, create new scenarios in order to determine if a free market approach or a governmental interventionist approach would have produced similar, better, or worse results.[278]

---

[277] Sarel, "Growth in East Asia: What We Can and What We Cannot Infer."

[278] Sarel, "Growth in East Asia: What We Can and What We Cannot Infer."

Despite the lack of consensus among economists and political thinkers of why certain countries in Asia maintained steady and high economic growth rates from the 1960s into the 1990s, there are some features that they did share, as pointed out by Thomas M. Leonard:

> [These countries had the following characteristics: a] focus on exports to rich industrialized nations, sustained rate of double-digit growth for decades, non-democratic and relatively authoritarian political systems during the early years, high tariffs on imports, undervalued national currencies, trade surplus, and a high savings rate.[279]

What is interesting in these observations is that Asian countries grew by exporting goods to wealthy nations while maintaining a semi-authoritarian political system. In other words while these countries allowed economic freedom in order to efficiently export goods they did not, to varying degrees, allow comparable political freedom.

China: Mao Ze Dong and Deng Xiaoping

China is a non-Asian Tiger country which is currently semi-authoritarian. Its semi-authoritarian political system differs from its previous highly authoritarian political model under Mao Zedong (1893-1976). Mao Zedong was a communist who followed Lenin's and Stalin's version of socialism but with a difference. The similarity he shared with Lenin and Stalin is that all three viewed themselves as hard socialists who were willing to take violent means to attain

---

[279] Thomas M. Leonard, *Encyclopedia of the Developing World* Volume I, A-E (New York: Routledge, 2006), 816.

political ends.[280] Mao's well-known quotation "Political power comes from the barrel of a gun" reflects his hard socialism. Mao differed from Lenin and Stalin in the persons whom he identified as the main revolutionary people to be directed by party leaders. In Maoism, peasants are the principle revolutionaries. In Leninism, factory workers are.

Mao came to power after the Qing dynasty fell from power in 1911 to revolutionaries. The following year, in February of 1912, the Qing emperor officially renounced his power. Yuan Shikai then began governing China as a president. Yuan had served in the Qing court and had fought against the revolutionaries. The revolutionaries agreed to stop fighting if the emperor stepped down and Yuan became president. While in office, Yuan became dissatisfied with his role. This led him to announce in August of 1915, despite protests, that he was emperor of China. Before he could consolidate power in himself he died in June 1916. After his death, China entered into a phase of political fragmentation in which the country was ruled in theory by a quick succession of presidents and in fact by competing warlords. When warlords needed food or money, a common way they obtained these goods was by raiding villages, stealing from them, and at times killing whomever they wished.[281]

During the time of the Yuan Shikai's rule and the warlords' rule, Sun Yatsen tried to unite China under his leadership. Sun Yatsen was backed by revolutionaries, and

---

[280] In 1919, Lenin invited left-wing socialists to join the Soviet Communist party to forming a Third International (the Communist International or Comintern). The Third International committed itself to a worldwide revolution in order to have factory workers be the world rulers.

[281] Patricia Ebrey, Anne Walthall, and James Palais, *East Asia: A Cultural, Social, and Political History* (Belmont: Wadsworth, 2009), 405-407.

he looked to Russia's communist leaders for guidance, specifically the Communist International founded by Lenin. In 1925, shortly before a unifying military movement called the Northern Expedition, Sun Yatsen died. In 1927, one of his most prominent disciples, Chiang Kaishek gained control over China and ruled it as the head of the Nationalist party from 1927 to 1949. During Chiang Kaishek's reign, China experienced a Civil War (1947-1949) between Chiang Kaishek's Nationalist Kuomingtang party and the Communist Party of China, headed by Mao Ze Dong.[282]

The Communist Party of China that Mao joined was founded in 1921 with the aid the Soviet's Communist International. The following year, the Communist Party united forces with the Nationalist Party. Together as the United Front they fought against China's warlords. Their alliance ended in 1927, the same year Chiang Kaishek became head of the Nationalist Party. From 1927 to 1930, the Chinese Communists, who were viewed as social agitators, were persecuted by the Nationalist Party. As a result, thousands of communists were executed. Survivors fled and hid from the Nationalists. Mao hid with his peasant communist followers in the Hunan mountains. While Mao and his communists looked to the Soviet Union for inspiration, Chiang looked for guidance from the Nazi fascists in Germany.[283] He even once said, "Fascism is…a stimulant for a declined, stagnant society. Can Fascism save China? We answer: Yes! Fascism is what China now most needs. At the present stage of China's critical situation, Fascism is a wonderful medicine exactly suited to China, and

---

[282] Ebrey, Walthall, and Palais, 415-426.
[283] Ebrey, Walthall, and Palais, 428-430.

the only tonic that can save it."[284]

In 1934, Mao led his followers in a retreat from the Nationalists. This over six thousand mile retreat is famously called the Long March, during which only about 8,000 survived out of original 86,000.[285] During the Second Sino-Japanese War (1937-1945), the Nationalists and the Communists, as requested by Stalin, once again were united in order to fight against the common enemy of Japan. During World War II, the Nationalists and the Communists collaborated with one another and with the Allies. The Communists naturally continued their relationship with the Soviet Union, which had joined the Allies during World War II. The Nationalists looked to the U.S. for guidance and support, specifically in how to defend against Japanese aggression. After World War II, tensions between the Nationalists and Communists were reignited in a Civil War (1947-1949). The war ended with Mao ruling China, and Chiang Kaishek ruling Taiwan.[286]

Mao sought guidance from the Soviet Union, specifically from Joseph Stalin from whom he asked advice. Mao's goal was to rapidly industrialize China. Following the Soviet model, Mao taxed farmers in order to finance his rapid industrialization plan. The Soviets supported his efforts by providing China with technical training and with loans.[287] In 1956, when the Soviet Union was ruled by Nikita Krushchev, Mao distanced himself from Stalin's repressive political style. One way he did this was his "Let a hundred flowers bloom" campaign in which people, in particular, intellectuals were encouraged to voice their criticism. The following year many

---

[284] J A Mangen, *Superman Supreme: Fascist Body as Political Icon – Global Fascism* (London: Routledge, 2000), 207.

[285] Ebrey, Walthall, and Palais, 434.

[286] Ebrey, Walthall, and Palais, 435-440.

[287] Ebrey, Walthall, and Palais, 458.

of those who publicly made their criticisms known were deemed unfit for promotions, and others were even sent to work in the countryside.[288]

In 1958, massive working communes were created in the countryside with the hope that China would experience a "Great Leap Forward". In these collectives, life was highly regulated as workers farmed and produced steel. Unfortunately, the work was poorly supervised resulting in low quality, unusable steel, and ruined farming soil. From 1959 to 1962, a terrible famine occurred which was responsible for around 30 million deaths. During the famine, relations between Khrushchev and Mao became strained and greatly reduced. For this reason, during the Vietnam War, Mao did not help the North Vietnamese who were funded and aided by the Soviet Union.[289]

In 1966, Mao attempted to reawaken the revolutionary movement which he feared was being compromised by Western capitalistic thought. This reawakening was called The Cultural Revolution (1966-1976). During this time, Mao's Red Guard set out to destroy anything deemed foreign to China or representing the culture and customs of the past. Libraries, museums and private homes were searched and items deemed anti-revolutionary were destroyed. The reputations of people deemed as anti-revolutionary were also destroyed in public denunciation meetings. Sometimes, these denunciation meetings included public beatings before crowds of people. The Cultural Revolution finally ended in 1976 upon the death of Mao.[290]

Following Mao's death, the prominent communist official Deng Xiaoping, who had been demoted by Mao,

---

[288] Ebrey, Walthall, and Palais, 465.
[289] Ebrey, Walthall, and Palais, 466-468.
[290] Ebrey, Walthall, and Palais, 468-473.

received his authority back. Deng gradually gained greater influence in the communist party. In 1978, he became China's foremost party leader. In 1998, he shifted China away from Mao's highly planned economic model to one that was partly privatized and partly state owned and directed. To allow greater privatization of China's economy, Deng ended collective farms, and allowed families to own their own land. He also privatized some state-owned businesses. Foreign investors were also invited into China under his leadership. The current Chinese constitution reflects Deng's revision of China's politics and economics. Under his authority, the constitution was reworded to define China as a "socialist market economy."[291] The chart below demonstrates Deng's reforms on China's economic growth. Despite allowing greater economic freedom and more political and religious freedom, though, China still maintains authoritarian, state-centered socialistic policies, as was evident in June 4th, 1989, governmental crackdown in Tiananmen Square,[292] the setting of its currency at an artificially lower rate of exchange,[293] and its insistence that Catholic bishops are chosen by the government.

---

[291] Patricia Buckley Ebrey, *The Cambridge Illustrated History of China,* Second Edition (Cambridge: Cambridge University Press, 2010), 333, 336.

[292] The Chinese Government claims 241 protestors were killed during the Tiananmen Square repression. This contrasts with the the then Soviet Union estimate of 10,000 killed, and also with the Chinese Read Cross estimate of 2,600 killed. Andrew Langley, *Tiananmen Square: Massacre Crushes China's Democracy Movement* (Mankato: Compass Point Books, 2009), 16.

[293] Wayne M. Morrison, and Jonathan E. Sanford, *China's Currency and Economic Issues* (New York: Nova Science Publishers, 2006), 4-5.

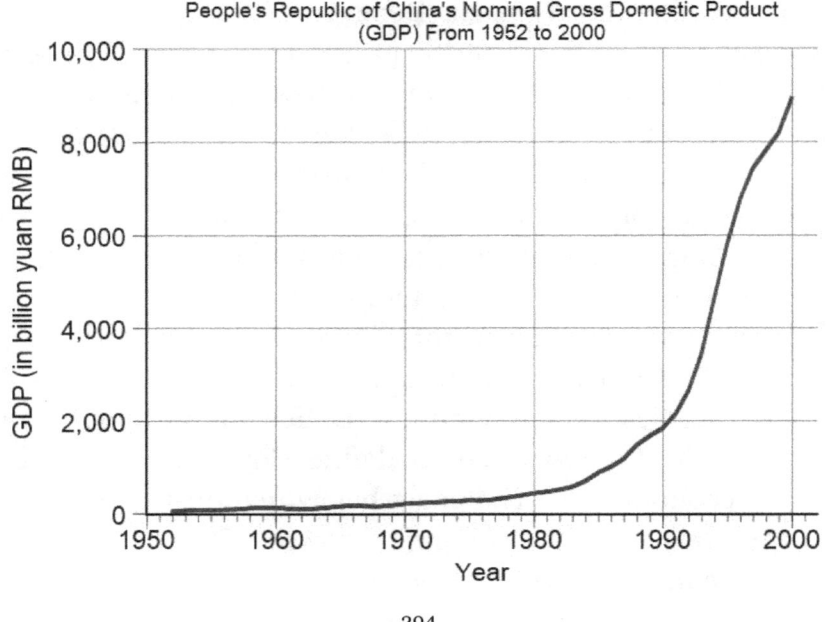

North Korea and Vietnam

North Korea never transitioned from the hard communist style of Joseph Stalin. Following World War II, as mentioned previously, the Soviets under the direction of Stalin occupied North Korea. One of the Koreans leaders during the Soviet occupation of Korea was Kim Il-sung. Kim Il-sung served the Soviet Army as the commander of a Korean first battalion of the 88th independent brigade.[295] In 1945, the Soviets chose Kim Il-sung to rule the Stalinist communist regime they

---

[294] Delphi234, "GDP of China in RMB from 1952 to 2000," chart, http://commons.wikimedia.org/wiki/File%3AGDP_of_China_in_RMB_from_1952_to_2000.svg (accessed March 5, 2015).

[295] Andrei Lankov, *The Real North Korea: Life and Politics in the Failed Stalinist Utopia* (Oxford: Oxford University Press, 2013), 2.

established in North Korea.²⁹⁶ Stalin was even responsible for editing the 1948 North Korean Constitution by which Kim Il-sung ruled. Kim Il-sung's reign over North Korea (Democratic People's Republic of Korea) lasted from 1948 to the day he died in 1994. In 1956, about three years after Stalin's death, Kim Il-sung distanced himself from the Soviet Union.

Khrushchev's attempt to de-Stalinize the Soviet Union disturbed Kim Il-sung and his cabinet since part of Khrushchev's plan was to decrease the cult of personality that Stalin had fostered. The fear was that Kim Il-sung's personality cult might also begin being questioned by North Koreans if their country continued their strong alliance with the Khrushchev-led Soviet Union.²⁹⁷ Kim Il-sung was succeeded by his son Kim Jong-il, who ruled from 1994 to 2011, the year he died. He, in turn was succeeded by his son Kim Jong-un. All three ruled according to Stalin's brutal, ruthless, and personality cult driven manner. They also all shared a common goal of being a military superpower. Below is an excerpt from the Korean woman Yeonmi Park, who in 2009 escaped from North Korea when only fifteen years old. The excerpt reveals the strong military and repressive culture of North Korea:²⁹⁸

> My father went into the military sometime around 1980 ... But less than a year after my father joined the army, he got very sick with a burst appendix ... [H]is military service was over for good. This could have been a catastrophe for him, because North Korean men without

---

[296] Lankov, 4.
[297] Lankov, 18.
[298] Yeonmi Park, *In Order to Live: A North Korean Girl's Journey to Freedom* (New York: Penguin Press, 2015), 4.

military backgrounds are usually shut out of the best jobs. ... [D]isaster struck in 1980 when Dong Il [her uncle] was accused of raping one of his students and attempting to kill his wife. ... In North Korea, if one member of the family commits a serious crime, everybody is considered a criminal. Suddenly my father's family lost its favorable social and political status. There are more than fifty subgroups within the main *songbun* castes, and once you become an adult, your status is constantly being monitored and adjusted by the authorities. A network of casual neighborhood informants and official police surveillance ensures that nothing you do or your family does goes unnoticed. Everything about you is recorded and stored in local administrative offices and in big national organizations, and the information is used to determine where you can live, where you can work. With a superior *songbun*, you can join the Workers' Party, which gives you access to political power. You can go to a good university and get a good job. With a poor one, you can end up on a collective farm chopping rice paddies for the rest of your life. And, in times of famine, starving to death.[299]

Unlike North Korea, Vietnam chose to follow the example set by Deng Xiao Ping and, consequently, shed much of its Soviet era influence. Reform of its hard style communism became very evident in 1986 when the Vietnamese communist government instituted economic and political reforms that enabled Vietnam to be more integrated in the world, politically and economically. These reforms are called the renovation or *doi moi* policy. The terminology to explain

---

[299] Yeonmi Park, *In Order to Live: A North Korean Girl's Journey to Freedom* (New York: Penguin Press, 2015), 26.

the policy at first was that Vietnam was to be "a socialist-oriented multi-sector operating along a market mechanism under state management." This was soon abbreviated to "a socialist-oriented market economy."[300] Since the *doi moi* policy was implemented, Vietnam has experience continued economic growth rates with some exceptions, such as from 1997 to 1998 when Asia underwent a region-wide financial crisis.[301] On January 11th, 2007, Vietnam's continued economic development allowed it to join the World Trade Organization.[302]

Quiz 12

1. (8 Points) Describe two reasons with specific examples why the "Asian Tigers" have been able to sustain their economic growth. Also, speculate why a similar phenomenon has not occurred in other developing nations. In your response distinguish between economic reform and political reform. To what extent did these two types of reform come together in the Asian Tiger countries?

---

[300] Vincent Edwards and Anh Phan, M*anagers and Management in Vietnam: 25 Years of Economic Renovation (doi moi)* (New York: Routledge, 2013), 22.

[301] Edwards and Phan, 23-34.

[302] "Vietnam and the WTO," wto.org, https://www.wto.org/english/thewto_e/countries_e/vietnam_e.htm (accessed March 6, 2016).

2. (9 Points) Compare and contrast China under Mao Ze Dong and China under Deng Xiaoping. Include the following in your answer: Stalin, role of peasants, Communism, Fascism, Great Leap Forward, Cultural Revolution, Cult of Personality, privatization, and Tiananmen Square.

3. (6 Points) Compare and contrast North Korea with Vietnam. Include the following in your answer: Stalin, Khrushchev, Cult of Personality, North Korean War, Vietnam War, and *doi moi*.

www.ingramcontent.com/pod-product-compliance
Lightning Source LLC
Chambersburg PA
CBHW031319160426
43196CB00007B/582